— THE COMPLETE —
BOOK *of* HERBS

THE COMPLETE
BOOK *of* HERBS

A Practical Guide to Cultivating, Drying, and
Cooking with more than 50 Herbs

Emma Callery

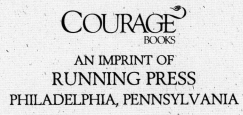

COURAGE
BOOKS

AN IMPRINT OF
RUNNING PRESS
PHILADELPHIA, PENNSYLVANIA

A QUINTET BOOK

Copyright © 1994 Quintet Publishing Limited.

This edition first published in the United States in
1994 by Courage Books, an imprint of
Running Press Book Publishers

9 8 7 6 5 4 3 2
Digit on the right indicates the number
of this printing

Reprinted 1995

Library of Congress
Cataloging-in-Publication Number
93–85549

ISBN 1–56138–351–1

This book was designed and produced by
Quintet Publishing Limited
6 Blundell Street
London N7 9BH

Creative Director: Richard Dewing
Designer: Nicky Chapman
Project Editor: Katie Preston
Editor: Emma Callery
Illustrators: Rowan Clifford, Chris Dymond

Typeset in Great Britain by
Central Southern Typesetters, Eastbourne
Manufactured in Singapore
by Eray Scan Pte Ltd
Printed in Singapore
by Star Standard Industries (Pte) Limited

Published by Courage Books
an imprint of Running Press Book Publishers
125 South Twenty-second Street
Philadelphia, Pennsylvania 19103–4399

CONTENTS

Introduction

People have made use of herbs since the beginning of time. Even before they learned to hunt, primitive people depended on herbs for both food and medicine, using them to add flavor to grain-based dishes and, later, as preservatives for meat and fish. Herbs were regarded so highly they assumed importance in religious rites and festivals, and many superstitions grew up around them.

The earliest record of the use of herbs is an Egyptian papyrus, dating from around 2000 BC, that mentions the existence of herb doctors, while it is known that herbs played an important role in all of the world's ancient civilizations. In India and China, where herbal remedies formed a large part of medicinal practice, many ancient remedies are still prescribed today by natural healers and practitioners of holistic medicine. The works of the great philosophers and physicians of Ancient Greece – Hippocrates in the third century BC with his

Right:

A painting of a late fourteenth century herb garden, showing the formality of the geometric design popular in medieval times.

herbal, *De Materia Medica*, and Dioscorides, *c* AD 60 – put hundreds of herbs into their botanical and medicinal context; and herbs are frequently mentioned in both the Old and New Testaments of the Bible. The Romans made such lavish use of herbs in both medicines and highly spiced dishes, the plants were an indispensable part of their equipment wherever they traveled. Indeed, it is said the success of the advancing Roman armies was attributed largely to their knowledge and use of herbs. All countries once Roman colonies have the Romans to thank for many of the herbs grown and used there today. The Roman scholar Pliny (AD 23–79) documented the extensive use of herbs in his many books on medicinal plants.

With the decline of the ancient cultures, the use of herbs passed into oblivion, only to re-emerge in the Middle Ages when they were cultivated in monastries and in the gardens of great estates. The monks put herbs to both medicinal and culinary use, and eventually the knowledge spread into the

Left:
An early twentieth-century engraving by F Delpech, after Vernet, shows a street herb seller offering sheaves of bay leaves and strings of garlic.

Far left:
Illustrated herbals abounded in the eighteenth century. This illustration is taken from a book by T Sheldrake published in 1759, called Botanicum medicinale.

towns and villages so people could grow their own self-help remedies. In the grander houses, herbs were used for pot-pourri as well as for strewing on floors to sweeten the atmosphere.

During this time many erudite works were written and published, setting out the characteristics and uses of a great many herbal plants. William Turner (1508–79), a doctor and a clergyman, wrote a comprehensive *Herball* based on his scientific background. John Gerard (b 1545), a versatile man who was the keeper of Lord Burghley's gardens, a surgeon, and apothecary to James I, wrote his *Herball* from practical experience. He formed a collection of medicinal and other plants from all over the world, and wrote about them with passion and understanding. And then there was Nicholas Culpeper, whose herbal set out to identify the medicinal plants and define their uses. He was a follower of a form of natural healing known as the Doctrine of Signatures, which teaches that like cures like; that red flowers, for example, are most likely to cure disorders of the blood.

Already well established in the medicine chest, herbs gradually came to be used more and more in cooking – as flavorings, in sauces, as preservatives, and as vegetables. This knowledge of the use of herbs spread throughout Europe, and was taken to North America by the early settlers. Here, it was the Shaker communities that first made a successful commercial enterprise out of growing and drying, and then selling their herbs.

By the nineteenth century, the use of herbs had fallen into decline. People no longer needed to grow herbs for domestic medicines when they could buy synthetic substitutes in the form of modern drugs. With modern storage and preserving techniques, herbs were no longer needed to preserve food, nor to mask undesired flavors, and people simply stopped growing them. Indeed, until only recently, four easy to grow herbs – parsley, thyme, mint, and chives – represented the sum total of most herb gardens.

Times have changed, the pendulum has swung back, and there is currently a strong revival of interest in these versatile plants. People have again become aware of the advantages of natural produce grown in an organic way. Cooks are ever more adventurous, experimenting with a wide range of exotic dishes requiring a large variety of herbs to flavor them. Not since the Middle Ages has there been such a wealth of interest in growing and using herbs. It is hoped this book will provide the inspiration to encourage this interest still further.

Right:

A pretty herb garden consisting of a clipped box "grid."

Growing Herbs

Growing herbs is one of the most delightful aspects of gardening. The plants are pleasantly fragrant, mostly decorative, some are highly colorful, and the majority can be used in the kitchen or around the home. Added to that, herbs are among the easiest plants to grow, so herb gardening is the ideal springboard for new and inexperienced gardeners.

Most herbs originate in the sunny climate of the Mediterranean and other hotspots around the world, and have been reluctantly introduced to colder climes. This being the case, the first requirement is to find a sunny spot for them where, if possible, they can be in the sun for at least five or six hours a day. There are a few shade-loving herbs specified in the Directory in the later pages of this book (pages 53–126), and these can be planted in the shadow of taller plants, or beside a wall or fence.

If you live in an area where cold winds are a more frequent feature than warm sunshine, this does not mean you cannot grow herbs successfully. Choose the most sheltered spot you can find, erect some kind of windbreak if you can, and be prepared to cosset tender young plants under a glass or plastic cloche or frame.

Preparing the Ground

The way you prepare the ground will have a significant effect on the health and quality of your plants for years to come, so it is well worth taking a little time and trouble at this stage.

Good soil is essential for the success of most plants, although there are a few that are so persistent, they will flourish even in poor, under-nourished soil. Most herbs have a common dislike, that of sitting in damp soil with their roots permanently wet, so good drainage is essential. You can easily test the effective drainage of your soil by watering it and taking note. If the water remains on the surface and does not sink in, the soil has too much clay. If, on the following day, the soil is wet only to the surface 1 inch, then chances are it is too sandy.

If you are starting a herb garden from scratch, you should first dig it over to a depth of 12 inches, the comfortable depth achieved with a garden shovel. If possible, dig in a 6 inch layer of compost or peat moss to improve the aeration of the soil and redress any deficiences. This helps to hold the moisture in sandy soils and facilitates drainage in heavy clay, thus giving the roots air – the oxygen they need – and room to grow. If drainage is very poor, add perlite granules in the proportion recommended on the packet.

Most herbs have one further preference, that of a neutral or slightly alkaline soil. If you happen to know the pH factor of your soil, herbs like it to be around 6 to 7½. If you do not know where your soil stands on this soil-test gauge, but suspect it is over-acid, dig in some lime with the humus. Also, to get the herbs off to the best possible start, it is best to add in a dressing of organic fertilizer; there are several environment-friendly brands on the market now, and most garden centers have a good selection.

Right:

Closely planted clusters of colorful herbaceous flowers, soft hummocks of aromatic plants and the juxtaposition of contrasting leaves make for a lively border packed with interest.

Plants or Seeds

Once you have made your selection of the plants you want to grow, there is one more decision to take: whether to buy nursery-grown plants or to ask friends for root divisions, layered stems, and so on.

In general, annuals are the quickest and easiest to grow from seed. At its simplest, you plant the seed in pots, trays, or a well-prepared seed bed once the soil has warmed up in spring, water it well, and the seedlings will appear a few days later. But even so, you might prefer the concept of "instant gardening," and opt to buy plants of annuals as well as others.

If you decide to grow from seed, you can choose whether to sow the seed outside in a prepared seed bed or inside in pots or trays. A seed bed should be completely free of weeds and rocks, and raked until the soil is fine and crumbly – what gardeners call a "fine tilth." To sow seeds outside in spring, it is essential to wait until there is no further danger of frost, and until the soil has had several days of sun to warm it. You can cheat a little by placing glass or plastic cloches over the soil before planting; this traps all the heat and does a good job of warming the soil.

By sowing seeds inside, either in the home or in a greenhouse, you can advance the date by two or three weeks, thus getting the seedlings established earlier. You can sow seeds in seed trays or in pots. Peat pots or peat blocks are ideal, especially for new gardeners: once the seedlings are established, they can be set out in the garden as they are, complete, without disturbing the roots. With trays or regular pots, use any good potting compost and be sure it is evenly moist. One way to do this is to cut a corner of the bag and pour in water, working it in to thoroughly dampen the soil – a horticultural game of mud pies. Fill the pots with the damp compost to within ½ inch of the top, and press it down gently. All roots need lightly compressed soil to enable them to take hold. Sow the seeds at the depth directed on the packet, rake a little soil over the top, and pat it down well. When sowing very fine seed, mix it with a little dry sand to distribute it evenly and guard against sowing too thickly.

Stand pots on a waterproof tray of sand or granules. Cover both seed trays and pots with a sheet of plastic to help retain moisture, and water them daily, so they never dry out. Remove the plastic covering once the seedlings appear, and put them in the sunniest place you can find. When the seedlings have taken root, you can water pots from below, pouring water into the trays rather than over the pots.

Thin the seedlings so that those remaining have a chance to develop as fully as possible, and prick out those growing in seed trays into pots. There should be about 1 inch of compost all around the roots.

SOWING SEEDS INSIDE

1. Gather together everything you need, clean pots, compost, seeds, and labels, before you start.

4. Make sure that you do not sow the seeds too thickly, so that the seedlings will be over-crowded when they germinate.

2. Put in a layer of broken crocks, then loosely fill the pots with compost and lightly firm it to within ¼ inch of the rim.

5. Sprinkle a thin layer of compost to cover the seeds and to keep them permanently moist but not soaking.

3. Tip some seeds into your hand and sow them thinly over the surface, or shake them evenly from the corner of the packet.

6. Use a fine sprinkler for watering. Cover the seeds with a piece of glass or plastic and keep them warm.

DIVIDING PLANTS

Right:

*To divide a clump of chives,
you can remove small,
well-rooted pieces from the
side to form new plants.*

Far right:

*Set out the new plants
about 1 foot apart to grow
into mature clumps.*

Right:

*Another way is to tease the
clump apart and make
several or many new
plants.*

At this stage, the seedlings benefit from a light feed with half-strength organic fertilizer every other day. Once they have developed two pairs of leaves, pinch out the tops to encourage bushy growth and the formation of branches. When the plants are several inches high and look healthy and strong, accustom them to the great outside by putting them in the garden, on the balcony, or in front of an open window for several hours a day, bringing them in at night. After several days of this half-in and half-out procedure, they will be ready to be planted out in their permanent home.

Even nurseries do not achieve 100 per cent perfection with their pot-grown plants so, if you are buying plants, make your selection carefully. Choose plants that are evenly colored – discoloring is a sign of weakness and poor health – and free from insects. Whitefly, for example, is a persistent predator, and you can do without introducing it to your garden or home on an imported plant. Also, look for plants with strong stems and several branches which will continue to perform well.

If you are uncertain about the fragrance of a plant, and are not sure you want to include it in your selection, brush the leaves lightly with your hand to release the scent. Do not pinch a leaf, this can cause bruising.

Finally, make sure all the plants you buy are clearly labeled before you leave the garden center or nursery. Several herbs have similar leaves, and if you are not yet familiar with the individual aromas, confusion can quite easily arise.

Setting plants out in the garden gives them something of a culture shock so it is important to do it at the right time of day. Hot sun causes the plants to wilt so much they may take days to recover, so transplant them on a cloudy day or, in a hot spell, early in the morning or late in the afternoon. Dig holes for the incoming plants and water them well so the plants immediately have one of their main requirements for healthy growth – a supply of moisture.

If you are using regular pots and not peat pots, take care to keep intact the maximum amount of soil around the roots of each plant. To do this, tip the pot upside down to release the roots and soil and hold it in your hand. If the roots look bunched together, gently ease them out at the sides, still keeping soil around them. Set each plant in its hole, with the top of the roots only just below the level of the ground. Press a little soil around the roots and give them a light sprinkling of water. Now fill the hole with more soil, pack it around the plant so the roots can get a good hold, and water again. Continue to water the plants frequently until new leaves appear. This indicates that the roots have become established, and all is well.

To plant herbs in containers, place a layer of broken earthenware (such as pieces of broken flower pots) in the bottom and fill the vessel to within 1 inch of the rim with a good quality potting compost. Then plant the herbs in the way described above.

Above, left:
A small group of culinary herbs planted at random in the kitchen garden; allium, mint, and summer savory.

Above:
Part of the miniature formal herb garden at the American Museum, Bath, England, which is contained in a small plot with a beehive at the center.

Above:
A narrow border at the base of a sunny wall affords the opportunity to start a limited collection of herbs. The beginner can be assured of success however limited the available space.

Right:
Block planting of herbs gives a patchwork effect, which may be extended or varied from one season to the next.

Propagation

Woody perennial herbs and shrubs can be grown from layered shoots and cuttings, far quicker than growing from seed.

Select leggy shoots of sage and, while they are still attached to the plant, make a few nicks at intervals along their length, using a sharp knife. Place them along the ground and peg at intervals, using staples of bent wire. Lightly cover the shoots with soil, and they will produce roots along their length. You can then cut the shoots away from the parent plant, and, if you wish, transplant each small, rooted plant to another site or give them to friends.

Layering roots or, more accurately, rhizomes of mint at the end of summer, is a similar technique, and one that enables you to enjoy fresh young leaves of mint throughout the winter.

Lift one root at the end of summer and cut a few of the rhizomes into short lengths, say about 6 inches. Lay them in a box of soil, cover lightly with more soil, and bring them inside. They will soon send out shoots and provide new leaf growth, far more aromatic than the toughened leaves on the plant at the end of the season.

Spring and early summer is the time to take cuttings of woody herbs such as thyme and rosemary. Tear off about 2 inches of new young growth to leave a "heel;" this gives far more successful results than cutting off the shoot with pruners. Insert the cuttings around the edge of a pot containing sandy soil, and press the growing medium firmly around the stems. Leave the cuttings to root, and keep them inside or under glass during the first winter. They can be planted out during the following spring.

Herbaceous perennials can be increased by taking root cuttings. Divide thick roots into 3-inch lengths. Plant them, straight side up, level with the soil surface, and cover with sand. Leave them in a closed frame for the winter.

To layer a shoot, select one close to the soil, making a slanting cut halfway through the underside of a stem opposite a bud or leaf joint on the upper side. Keep the cut open with a matchstick or a small rock, and anchor the layer in good soil with a hooked wire so that the cut faces the soil. Bend the tip upward. As soon as the layer is well rooted, cut it away from the parent stem.

TAKING A CUTTING

1. A healthy, well-developed plant can yield several cuttings. Use your discretion and do not cut it back too hard, or you will weaken the plant.

2. To take a cutting, make a slanting cut just under a leaf joint, about 4 inches from the tip. Strip off the lower leaves and stipules.

3. Dip the ends of each cutting in a hormone rooting compound and insert them around the rim of a pot of gritty soil. Water lightly.

Care and Maintenance

Herbs are fairly undemanding once they are established in the garden or in containers. The main task is to keep the area free of weeds, which can suffocate young plants. Harvesting the leaves and pinching out flowering shoots encourages more bushy growth.

Since most herbs originate from dry climates they do not need – and most do not want – rigorous watering, and they can survive long dry spells. However, you will soon see when they appear to be losing their freshness and are in need of a gentle soaking.

Perennial herbs, such as thyme and sage, tend to become woody, and the plants benefit from cutting back at the end of the season. Even so, there comes a time when they will not retain or regain their original compact shape, and therefore it is best to renew plants every few years.

Caring for plants in a container garden carries rather more responsibility, since they do not have their roots in the soil with all its natural ingredients to feed them. Water plants daily in a dry spell, and add an organic fertilizer at least every two weeks so they have adequate nourishment. If you are leaving shrubby plants such as bay to overwinter outside, protect the roots from frost by wrapping the whole container in sacking. It may not be aesthetically pleasing, but is a necessary and effective protection.

Keep inside herb plants in the sunniest spot you can find. In an ideal world, they like about five hours of sunlight or ten hours of strong artificial light a day. Turn the pots from time to time so the herbs do not grow unevenly towards the light, and inspect them regularly for insect attack. If you find insects on the plants, wash the leaves in soapy water or spray with an organic pesticide. Do not use chemical preparations on herbs you are just about to eat.

Left:

A small "parsley pot" with holes at intervals around its circumference makes an attractive planter for a windowsill. This one is planted with bay, mint and parsley.

Right:

A trio of sturdy pots closely planted with thyme makes an attractive feature on a pathway or the corner of a terrace.

Harvesting

The growing season for herbs is a comparatively short one, and the period during which the essential oils are at their richest even shorter. So the whole object of herb growing can be jeopardized if the harvesting and drying are not carried out properly. It is essential to know which part of the herb is required – seed, root, leaf, or the whole herb – and the time to gather it for best results. Sometimes the timing is critical. In general, leaves are richest in the essential oils just as the flowers begin to open; seeds have to be ripe but need to be caught before the plant sheds them; roots also have to be mature and "ripe." The correct time to collect each plant varies from garden to garden and season to season, and can be learned only by constant attention to detail and a little practical experience. Some sprigs of herbs may be picked for immediate use, fresh, like chives, mint, and parsley, whenever there are growing leaves available through the year.

For the amateur herb-grower, two factors are of primary importance. First, never collect more plant material than can be handled in the time and space available, and second, only harvest when the plants are dry. This is best done when the heavy dews have dispersed and before the heat of the day; often a gentle shake early in the morning will rid them of dew quite quickly as the temperature rises.

The object of drying herbs is to eliminate the water content of the plant quickly and, at the same time, retain the essential oils. Therefore it is sensible to harvest one plant quite separately from another and to do it in small quantities at a time. Plant material in baskets, boxes, or on sheets – however it is collected – soon wilts, warms up and begins to deteriorate. Deal with a small amount at a time and then return to the garden for more.

Above:

The ideal time to harvest herbs is after the morning dew has gone, but before the day becomes too warm. Here, thyme is being cut and collected in a clean dry garden trug. Always harvest healthy herbs when they are in the peak of condition and therefore richest in essential oils.

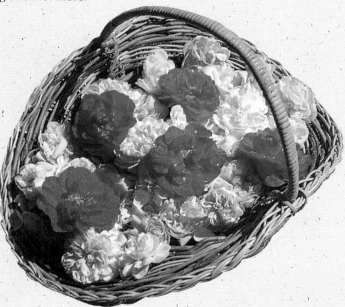

Right:

Rose heads cut from the plant just as they reach maturity are collected in a box or basket to avoid bruising the petals. Select and handle unblemished flowers with care and do not leave them together in the basket for longer than it takes to collect them as they will begin to warm up and deteriorate.

Top:

Seed needs to be ripe before harvesting. Examine the heads closely to be sure that all the seeds are ready. Here fennel is being inspected.

LEAVES

Unless a crop is being cleared, pick a few whole shoots from each plant so as not to jeopardize the plant's continued existence. Cut, rather than pull, them off cleanly and select only healthy insect- and disease-free shoots.

It is important to keep the shoots of one plant separate from those of another, even when, say, two kinds of mint are being harvested.

SEEDS

When seed is being saved for sowing it should be allowed to ripen on the plant and be collected only from well-grown, healthy plants. A muslin or thin paper bag popped over the whole inflorescence and secured with a plastic tie or rubber band will contain the seeds as they are released by the plant. Seed being saved for propagation needs to be stored in envelopes of aluminum (made by folding aluminum about

ROOTS

Most herb roots are plump and ripe for lifting in the autumn at the end of the growing season when they are richest in stored food. In general, yellow flag, elecampane, and aconite are ready in early fall; eryngo, Solomon's seal, golden heliotrope in the spring, and English mallow a little later.

Lift whole roots with a garden fork or flat-tined potato fork, taking care not to puncture or bruise the outer skin. Rub or wash them free of soil, cut back any residual top growth and fibrous rootlets, cut them into convenient sections or slices and then set them out to dry.

the seeds) or in small boxes with a secure lid, and labeled with their name and date of collection.

Where seeds such as caraway, sweet cicely or dill are destined for culinary use, the old flowering stems, or even the whole plant, can be pulled up. By hanging them upside-down in a shaded dry place the seeds will loosen of their own accord and can be collected in paper or cotton bags tied over the flower heads. Alternatively, they can be allowed to fall on to sheets of clean paper or cloth beneath. If the latter method is undertaken, particular care has to be exercised to keep the seeds of different plant species separate.

The ideal time to harvest herbs is after the morning dew has gone, but before the day becomes too warm. Here, thyme is being cut and collected in a clean dry garden trug. Always harvest healthy herbs when they are in the peak of condition and therefore richest in essential oils.

Holidays frequently coincide with seed ripening, so by covering flower heads with paper bags many seeds can be saved. Once ripe and collected, the seeds need to be separated from the chaff either by simple winnowing, sieving, or hand picking. In practice, tilting and shaking them onto a sheet of paper towel is a slow but sure way of getting the job done.

WHOLE HERB

It may be necessary to cut all the parts of a plant which are above ground, especially if the crop has been grown for harvesting. Parsley can be cut at any time when the plant is not in flower and fresh green leaves are available. Others need to be cut before the flowers bloom but after the leaves and shoots have reached their full size. Keep the plants separate, dealing with a limited amount of material at any one time.

BARK

Bark is usually shaved off branches in the fall and is then dried. The active elements vary in quantity according to season; homoeopathic medicine, for example, stipulates at what time of year bark should be cut. It is important not to leave large patches of bare wood when shaving bark off; it is better to prune whole branches and strip bark from them.

FLOWERS

Flowers are harvested mainly for their color, shape, and decorative attributes, and are used to embellish food and drink. Pick them just as they become perfectly formed, and avoid bruising and crushing the petals. Gather a few at a time on a baking tray or plate on which they can be separated with as little handling as possible. Lavender flowers gathered for lavender bags and rose buds for potpourri need to be picked while immature so they retain their shape and scent.

Some flowers may harbor earwigs or other insects; these can be floated out by dipping the flowers in water before using them. Whatever use the flowers are to be put to, it is important to deal with them immediately after picking. Flowers for crystallizing ought to be fresh or else they will fold together. Those for freezing can be quickly blanched in tiny bunches in boiling water, popped into a freezer bag, labeled and dated, and put into the freezer. Alternatively, a favorite mixture of herbs can be frozen together in bags in small quantities, so that they are ready for use without waste.

Large soft leaves, such as basil, should be oiled on each side – a good olive or sunflower oil will do – flattened between sheets of waxed or greaseproof paper, and then frozen. Another method is to put tiny sprigs of, for example, mint, marjoram, lemon balm, or thyme into an ice tray with water and freeze them in cubes. Herbs such as mint and borage can be chopped then frozen in cubes; single borage flowers set in ice cubes can be popped into drinks at a later date.

Above:

Pull apart the petals of harvested roses for quick and even drying, but leave a few buds intact to decorate potpourri. Roses destined for inclusion in potpourri are best dried together with other flowers, to help form a homogenous mixture where all the scents combine to make a rich fragrance.

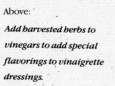

Above:

Add harvested herbs to vinegars to add special flavorings to vinaigrette dressings.

Making an Herb Garden

The golden rule for an herb garden is to keep it simple. European gardens in medieval times included the bulk of those plants which we today call herbs, and were then made up of a series of rectangular beds each containing one sort of plant. Today's version of this is the chess board idea of plant and pave, which is simplicity itself to make and manage.

Plant and Pave

The basic area to be cultivated is divided into squares, and each alternate square – corresponding to the black squares of the chess board – is set with a single paving slab, or turfed, or even bricked. The spaces remaining – the white squares of the board – can then be planted with one herb each: marjoram, mint, dill, caraway; use several plants of each herb according to the size of the square. Where space is limited, or in a newly acquired garden in which the whole site is not ready, a few alternate squares treated in this way represent the beginning of an herb collection. It can be extended later with more paving and more plants. It is a particularly useful style of garden for informal areas, or for filling in awkward corners, offering a transition from lawn or driveway to border, and at the same time providing something easy to maintain and pleasing to the eye.

Where different levels have to be negotiated, the same overall alternate paving style can be used, ranging one or two rows above another. The alternating square effect may also be created by placing square containers each devoted to a single kind of plant in this chess board fashion.

Right:

A contemporary print of a seventeenth century garden enclosed by railings with raised beds of various shapes containing herbs and other plants.

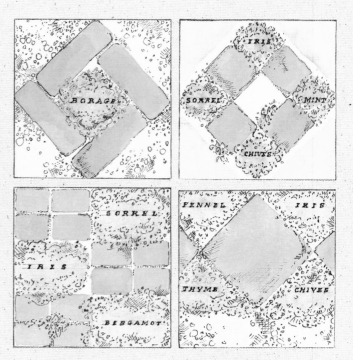

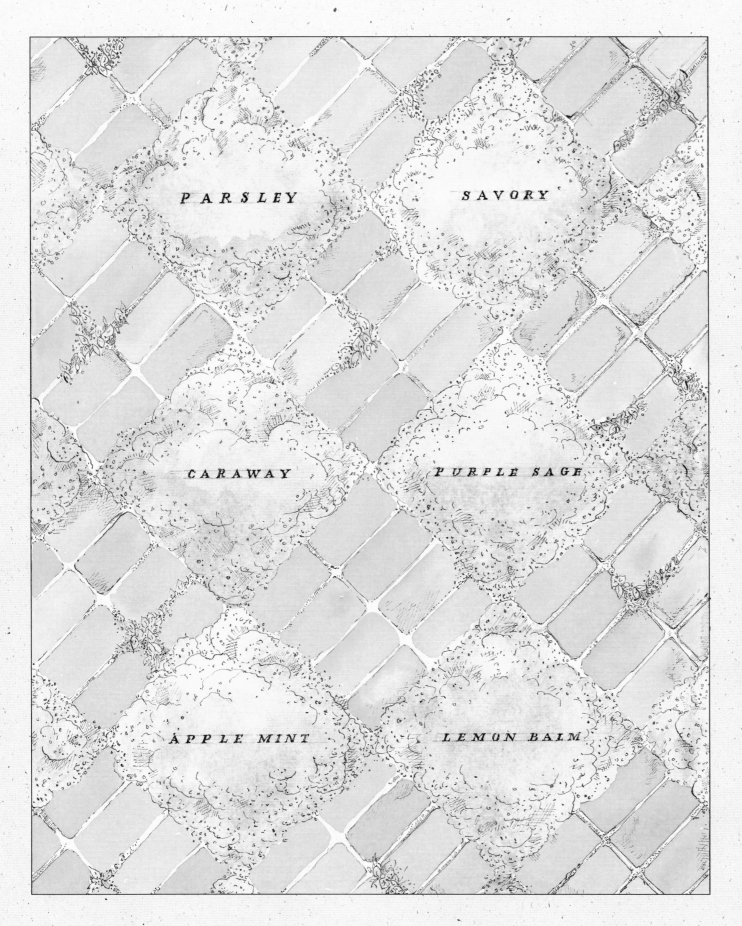

PARSLEY

SAVORY

CARAWAY

PURPLE SAGE

APPLE MINT

LEMON BALM

Left and opposite:

The simplicity of herbs is enhanced by some formal design. The cleanest is achieved by the use of square paving slabs, brick patterns or lawn turf, used alternately with the plants. With an uncomplicated design on a small scale there is no need to make heavy work of marking out the design. Canes or trails of sand or gravel will serve as a guide line. Time and effort spent in laying paving, and getting it level, or in creating warm effects with brick patterns for the basic design, is well spent in the herb garden. Plants can be varied from season to season, although the paving is permanent.

The possible variations on the theme of the basic chess-board idea are numerous, the only requisites being that the areas should be level and the pattern repetitive in both size and composition. Select plants that complement each other, either in flower color or leaf form and unless the area is extensive, avoid tall-growing herbs such as fennel and angelica.

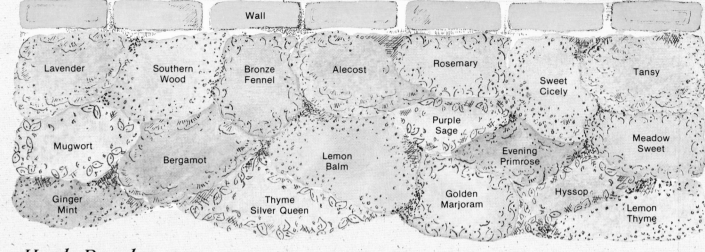

Wall

Lavender · Southern Wood · Bronze Fennel · Alecost · Rosemary · Sweet Cicely · Tansy

Mugwort · Bergamot · Purple Sage · Lemon Balm · Evening Primrose · Meadow Sweet

Ginger Mint · Thyme Silver Queen · Golden Marjoram · Hyssop · Lemon Thyme

Herb Borders

Simplicity of planting is the key to success for the herb border. The border itself ought not to be too wide to allow ease of access and is best backed by a wall, fence, or hedge to provide both shelter and good visual effect. Herbs themselves do not necessarily provide the most appropriate background hedge. A rose hedge is often too spreading, elder too hungry; rosemary, lavender and bay need protection themselves in all but the mildest areas and are not really winter hardy plants at all.

The less sophisticated the planting scheme the better, so that one plant will set off another or provide the complementary foil in leaf form, clump size or leaf color for its neighbors. Low-growing plants like thyme, chives, and marigolds need to be set towards the front of the border; the taller ones, like lovage, rosemary, fennel, angelica, at the back.

A formal effect in border planting can be introduced by making a formal edge with santolina, thyme, or golden marjoram, or by placing paving slabs in a diamond pattern near the front of the border. Both of these ideas are especially rewarding when set along paths crossing a sloping site, or alongside a flight of steps.

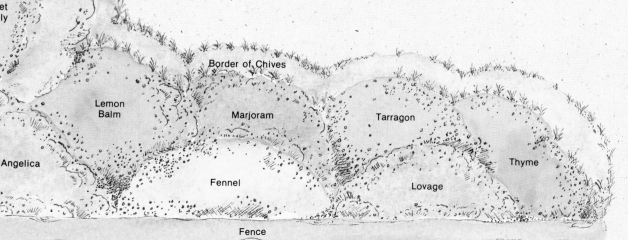

House

Sage · Mint

Borage · Sweet Cicely

Border of Chives

Lemon Balm · Marjoram · Tarragon

Angelica · Fennel · Lovage · Thyme

Fence

Above:

Herbs can be gathered easily, as and when required from an informal border along a pathway in a kitchen garden.

Left:

Culinary herbs assembled in a sunny corner near the house will provide a constant supply of fresh flavoring all through the summer. The depth of the border must be in proportion with the scale of the garden and an edging of slabs, a path or a lawn in front will add the trimness necessary to emphasize the abundance of the border. The tallest plants should be set at the back, with those of intermediate height in the middle and those of short stature in front.

Formal Designs

It has to be accepted that herbs can never be first class plants for dramatic garden effect. Their appeal lies in their Old World associations, their aroma and the very simplicity of the plants themselves. They have largely escaped the contriving hybridists. The most attractive herb gardens are therefore made by using a careful selection of herbs in a repeated design or a bold theme of formal beds. One of the simplest patterns can be achieved by setting wedge-shaped beds around a central feature to form a circular plot. Bricks set along the lines of the imaginary spokes and rim of a wheel produce a very satisfactory bed in which to plant radiating rows of herbs. Variations are possible too: fewer beds, octagonal plots, a central sundial, a beehive, or birdbath surrounded by paving or chamomile lawn all work well as the focal point in a formal circular garden. The next progressive is to set a square plot within it. Whenever possible, measure the plot first and draw out a general plan to scale on paper before marking it out on the ground. Once on the ground it is always a good idea to indicate paths and beds by rope or a garden hosepipe and to leave the design for a few days. This way, it can be viewed from the windows of the house, a wheelbarrow can be wheeled about to ensure that the paths can be negotiated, the sunlight and shadows can be watched, and mistakes can be avoided.

Beds should be large enough not to give a dotted effect and yet small enough to be workable. Whatever pattern or arrangement of beds is decided upon, the garden should be symmetrical for the best effect.

Quite unpromising sites can be transformed into herb gardens, which once established, need comparatively little attention during the growing season.

Top:
Borage florishes in a newly constructed raised bed. The blue flowers proclaim that this is the site for herbs next year.

Above:
Bold planting of herbs across a steep slope on either side of a flight of steps, demonstrates their decorative value. Great yellow-green mop heads of tall angelica at the back reduce the gradient visually and force the emphasis on to the hummocks of santolina at foot level.

Below left:
When space is limited, a level site can be formed into a wheel garden with rim and spokes of brick, tiles or wood. Or make a rainbow wheel: red, monarda; orange, marigold; yellow, tansy; green, lemon balm; blue, borage; indigo, basil "Dark Opal;" violet, peppermint.

Below:
Tile-like squares, each planted with a different herb, make a dainty arrangement for a restricted area. Confine each herb sufficiently to allow it to be reached from the surrounding pathway. If the planted area is to be an island bed, then the taller plants need to be set towards the center.

Hedge

Lavender

Culinary

Physic

Fennel

Lovage

Savory

Lungwort

Foxglove

Licorice

Caraway

Parsley

Yarrow

Feverfew

Sorrel

COBBLES

Poppy

Thyme

Germander

Self
Heal

Mint

Monkshood

Lavender

Hedge

Chamomile
Turf

Chamomile
Turf

Lily
of
the
Valley

Chamomile
Turf

Chamomile
Turf

Marjoram

Pepper-
mint

Germander

Germander

Thyme

Evening
Primrose

Lemon
Balm

Lavender

Solomon's
Seal

Iris

Apple
Mint

Dill

Hedge

Poke
Weed

Motherwort

Comfrey

Chives

Chervil

Bronze
Fennel

Physic

Hedge

Lavender

Culinary

Above:

Pretty and sweet scented, this small formal garden is planned to provide for a succession of culinary and physic plants. The surrounding lavender hedge forms the essential part of the integral design and it will take two or three years to become established. Space has been created at the center by keeping the levels low – chamomile lawn and low germander edging; then the plants rise irregularly to the four corners. The whole is embraced by the low lavender hedge; seen across a lawn or yard the herbs can be enjoyed at a distance, every bit as much as within the garden itself.

Knot Gardens

The most elaborately-designed formal gardens are made along the lines of the Elizabethan knot gardens, based upon some intricate pattern of beds and interlaced clipped outlines. The design is symmetrical and usually repetitive and is always seen at its best from higher levels of the surrounding garden or from a building.

Old gardening books often contain designs for knots; sixteenth and seventeenth century architecture and costume illustrations may suggest designs. Look for inspiration on ceilings, door panels, and badges, and transfer them to the ground. In Tudor gardens, the knots were probably composed of plants not all of which are today considered to be herbs. Low-growing plants such as sweet marjoram, hyssop, thyme, germander, santolina, and box were used to form the threads and outline of the design, and were close-clipped to maintain a crispness of presentation. Box was soon found to be one of the most successful, and today is most commonly employed as the formal edging to many herb beds in both kitchen gardens and decorative gardens.

In forming knots, the aim is to plant the herbs close together in chains and to encourage them to develop evenly to the same height; too much unevenness is quite unattractive. Once established, the ribbons of growth need to be clipped once or twice a year with hand shears. The spaces between the ribbons or chains can be filled with colored shale or pebbles (as was the practice in Tudor England), or they may be filled with low-growing young plants such as those suggested above.

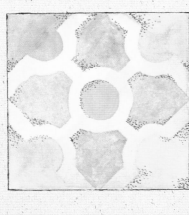

Above:
In practice, decorated tiles could suggest ideas for simple knot design. Limit the number of kinds of herb to three or four at the most.

Crest Diamonds in the paper I doe frame,
And in the ground I can draw the same.

Left:
Many garden writers of the seventeenth century suggested designs for knots. This design from Blake's The Complete Gardener's Practice *(1656) would not be too difficult to achieve.*

Left:
Part of a simple knot garden in the making. Chains of box and germander, interwoven, once established will be close clipped to make the pattern crisp.

Right:

Choose compact low-growing herbs to make the knot garden design featured here. Although it appears complicated and intricate, only three kinds of herb are used, say hyssop, germander, and box. (Thyme, santolina or lavender would be suitable also.) Plant them evenly and very close together to form ribbons. Once they are growing, clip them regularly to achieve a crisp uniform pattern, taking care to create an interlaced effect. Use colored rocks to fill the spaces.

Growing Herbs in Confined Spaces

Many gardens do not have areas appropriate for herb cultivation, perhaps because they lack light or shelter, or have a very heavy or sticky soil. Most herbs and aromatic plants can be perfectly successfully cultivated in containers – window boxes, troughs, decorative pots, or boxes. Suitable compost can be provided and the containers moved around or replenished regularly. A good trick is to sink pots with herb plants into the containers themselves and cover the pot rim with peat or pea gravel over the surface of the larger container. If a plant fails, or grows unattractive as the season progresses, its tiny pot can simply be removed and replaced with something else, and the gravel surface smoothed over as if nothing had happened. Instant gardening!

Rooted cuttings, or the little herb plants that can be bought in markets, should be tucked quite thickly into the larger containers and treated in the same way. Be prepared to change and replace plants that outgrow their allotted space or begin to grow awkwardly and spoil the effect. Remember that especially during warm weather, containers of all kinds need constant attention, particularly watering. Balconies, porches, and windowsills for office workers all provide perfectly suitable places in which to grow herbs in an assortment of containers, provided that sufficient light is available. Almost all plants need a minimum of five to six hours of good light at some time during the day.

The word "container" can be interpreted in the widest sense and can be applied to raised beds, or the tops of walls that surround, say, a patio. When plants are cultivated at waist level, older or disabled persons can also participate in gardening; if the raised beds are arranged thoughtfully, wheelchairs can be maneuvered between them and the disabled person can be a herb gardener too.

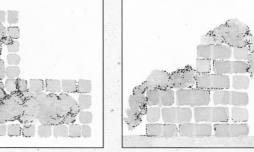

Far left:
A terracotta strawberry jar planted with artemisias and sage.

Left:
Herbs tumble from an eighteenth century lead water tank to create a miniature herb garden.

Left:
Side view and top view of raised bed design.

Right:
Specially built raised beds of brick or stone add a decorative dimension to the patio or yard. Herbs cultivated in this way, perhaps mixed in with other aromatic plants, bring the aromas nearer to nose level. A seat set in the side invites lingering.

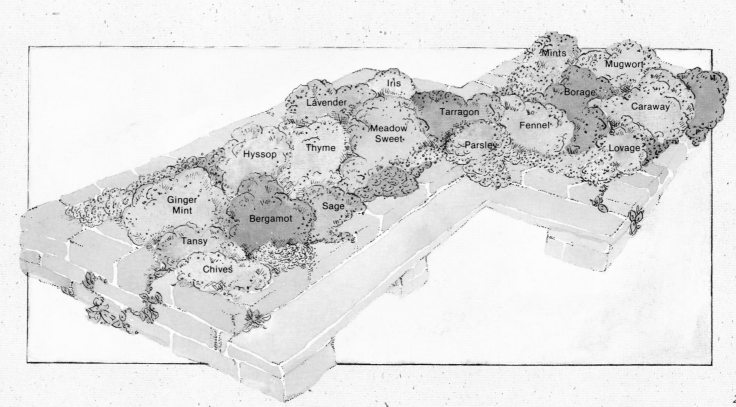

Right:

Individual herbs are not the best plants for garden decoration and for this reason they are always more effective when assembled together.

Various attractive schemes can be devised to enhance their decorative values. In this island bed, the central diamonds contain comfrey, licorice, motherwort, and foxglove, plants of medium height, and they are surrounded by lower-growing plants such as pulmonaria, yarrow, and pennyroyal. Consideration has also been given to the overall color effect, so that a blue-purple-pink theme emerges, supported by dusty grey and blue green. Repetition of a planting theme is always a positive approach to garden design, never more so than for herbs. Where space allows, these taller diamond shapes among the lower-growing herbs could be repeated. Variations on the color of the diamonds could be introduced, for example yellows, with tansy, evening primroses, variegated lemon balm, and fennel, with ginger mint; golden marjoram and variegated thyme would look pretty among the surrounding smaller plants.

Above:

A wooden wheelbarrow is an attractive container for a small herb garden.

Growing Herbs in Gravel

Above:

A simple container may be used as the central feature in a small herb garden, and height added by growing fennel in it.

Cultivating herbs in gravel gardens is becoming increasingly popular and has the great advantage of being labor saving. Choose good clean gravel or aggregate, or where available, washed rock chippings.

Relatively small areas can be turned into attractive herb gardens in this way. The area must be cleared of perennial weeds, forked over and leveled, then covered with stout black plastic sheeting. Cut holes in this wherever herbs are to be planted, and if young plants are not ready to plant out, push a stake or label into the soil beneath to indicate the position for later planting. Spread the gravel over the whole of the sheeting to a minimum depth of 3 inches, and rake it level. The sheeting will act as both weed barrier and mulch, retaining moisture in the soil. Drainage will only be a disadvantage in wet summers or where large areas have been covered.

A spray over the plants with water in the evening will suffice in all but the warmest of regions. Such a spray played over the whole area, plants, and gravel will heighten the perfume in the garden as the moisture evaporates.

Above:

Sweet bay is a favorite plant to grow in containers, but needs to be protected from winter winds. It makes a delightful evergreen decoration for a porch or garden room or sheltered balcony.

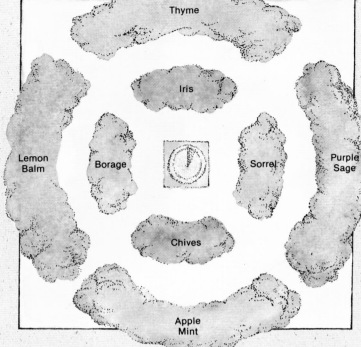

Top, above, and left:
Gravel makes good clean path material, needing little maintenance other than an occasional rake over to keep it neat and level. The whole area can be covered with gravel right up to the plants, to make a small area appear larger. Spread black plastic sheeting over the ground beneath the gravel to prevent weeds from growing through.

Using Herbs

Drying

No herb can be stored fresh. Much of the value and flavor of an herb can be lost by ineffective drying; if the properties and color of the herb are to be preserved, the whole drying process must be carried out as quickly and evenly as possible. Shade, air, and warmth are the essential requirements – constant temperature being the critical factor.

Herbs (grown and) dried at home, with a little care, can be far superior to most commercially available products. However, not all herbs dry equally satisfactorily – chives and fennel, for example, simply flop.

The simplest drying method is to tie each kind of herb separately into bunches. Each bunch should be tied loosely by the stems to allow air to circulate and left hanging freely. Hang them in a dry shaded place – attic, spare room, summer house, clean garden shelter, or barn. In drier, warmer climates, bunches of herbs can be hung outside in the shade, or in the high ceilings of a warm room with the windows open, or even in a bedroom where a breeze can be circulated through louvered shutters. This method of drying is difficult to control, however, and the end results are unpredictable.

Herb leaves are properly dried when they snap easily between the fingers and thumb. Some stems are slow to dry, so the dried leaves can be stripped off and stored and the stems abandoned. If herbs are stored before drying is complete, moisture will be reabsorbed from the atmosphere and the material will soon deteriorate.

CONTROLLED DRYING

Quicker and more consistent results can be obtained by spreading sprigs of herbs evenly over trays, box tops, or drying frames, or merely on to a table on sheets of paper. Keep the sprays of one kind of herb together and separate from the others. Sprigs are the easiest to handle – only large-leaved herbs like lovage and comfrey need to have their stripped stems removed before drying.

Drying frames should be made from some light porous material such as muslin or fine netting stretched over a rectangular wooden frame to allow air to circulate. The herbs need to be turned over by hand several times during the first two days.

Trays can be put into a linen closet or domestic boiler room and the doors left open.

ARTIFICIAL HEAT

For better results the drying process needs to be speeded up and controlled. Some artificial heating capable of maintaining an equable temperature, and some ventilation to keep the air moving, needs to be provided. For the first 24 hours, a temperature of about 90° needs to be maintained to reduce the water content as quickly as possible. The temperature can then be reduced to around 75° to complete the process. The whole process takes from three to six days if properly carried out.

MICROWAVE-DRYING

A more sophisticated method of drying – in a microwave – preserves plant materials in minutes rather than days. This method gives good results with clusters of flowers such as marjoram and lady's mantle, tansy and yarrow, cornflowers and chamomile, and with leaves such as lavender, sage, and purple sage, fennel, and rosemary. The method is simple. Cover the turntable or plate with a piece of paper towel, arrange the plant materials in a single layer, making sure that no two items are touching, and process them on low power for about 3 minutes. The actual processing time will vary according to the wattage of the microwave and the volume and density of the plant materials. Check every 30 seconds or so once they are almost ready and remove them as soon as they become crisp and papery. Even a few seconds too long will render them unmanageably brittle.

USING DESICCANTS

Drying plant materials in a desiccant greatly extends the range of decorative options open to you. The technique involves the use of a drying agent to draw out the moisture from the plant. To do this evenly and satisfactorily, the desiccant must come into contact with every part of the leaf or flower, filling every crevice and following every curve. Alum powder (aluminum sulphate) and household borax (sodium borate), both of which are available from drug stores, are most suitable for use with small subjects – borage flowers and the like. Ground silica gel crystals, which may be obtained from some drug stores, florists', and camera stores, give consistently good results with all but the most delicate of materials. Cornmeal has a similarly wide application, and dry silver sand can be used for the most substantial plant materials.

Silica gel crystals are probably the most versatile choice. The crystals are available in two forms – standard white and those that are color-indicating. The latter type are blue when dry and gradually change color through white to pale pink as they absorb moisture from the plant materials.

Used alone, both alum and borax tend to adhere to delicate petals and tiny leaves, and the crystals can be difficult to brush off the dry, brittle materials. Mixing one part silica gel crystals with two or three parts alum or borax makes the final brushing process easier.

Cut stems of leaf sprays so that they are short enough to be placed horizontally in a shallow container. The stems of flowers such as marigolds, pinks, and roses should be no more than 1 inch long. Spread a ½-inch layer of the desiccant into the container. Arrange leafy sprays flat and flowers upright in the crystals. Gently trickle the desiccant over the plant material so that each piece is completely covered. Add crystals until there is a ½-inch layer over the material.

If you are using the "cold" method, cover the container. If it does not fit tightly, seal it all around the edge with adhesive tape. Leave the container undisturbed for three days, then check every day until the plant material is dry enough to remove.

To use a conventional oven, set it to the lowest temperature and, if you are working with silica gel crystals alone, process the materials for 20-25 minutes, depending on the nature of the plant, and check at frequent intervals towards the end. If you use a mixture of silica gel crystals and any of the other desiccants, which are less efficient heat conductors, increase the processing time by about one half.

To use a microwave and a desiccant, process the materials in an uncovered container on low power for 6–7 minutes. The time will vary according to the properties of the microwave, the desiccant, and the plant material, and you should check on progress every minute or so. It is a good idea to make notes of the processing times you have found successful.

Leave heat-assisted desiccants to cool slightly for about 10 minutes, then carefully remove the dried materials. Brush the surface with a small, camel-hair or similar paint-brush and store the materials in a dry place in boxes between layers of tissue or paper towels.

Left:

Herbs may be dried in silica gel crystals in the microwave, in a conventional oven at the lowest setting or in a covered container, at room temperature. The plant materials to be dried should be completely submerged. When the herbs are dry, the silica gel crystals should be removed with a small, soft brush.

DRYING ROOMS

Where a considerable quantity of herbs is to be dried, or when dried herbs are being prepared for a market, it is worth considering creating a special drying cabinet.

The correct drying temperature must be achieved before the fresh herbs are taken in; and perhaps an extractor fan set high in the room will be needed to remove the moisture and keep the air moving. The warmer the air, the more moisture it can hold and this needs to be removed. The moisture content of most plants is above 70 per cent and the object of brisk drying is to change the condition of the leaf rather than its chemical content.

Trays can be fitted into specially constructed racks. If freshly gathered material has to be brought into the room where other herbs are still drying, the moisture drawn from the fresh material will be reabsorbed by the dry herbs. The trays of fresh herbs should therefore be placed high up in the room nearest the extractor fan.

RUBBING DOWN

Once the herbs have cooled down after drying, the rubbing down process can begin. This is best carried out in a well ventilated place, wearing gloves and a smog mask (if any quantity of material is to be handled). Hand pick the leaves from the stalks. Some, like marjoram, can be stripped simply by running the fingers along the stem. Discard the stalks and crush the leaves either in a domestic grinder or with a rolling pin or simply by rolling them up one kind at a time in a cloth and rubbing the cloth.

STORING

Once rubbed down, dried herbs need to be stored immediately in air-tight, dark containers to prevent them from picking up moisture again from the air. Glass jars are ideal if they are to be kept in a dark closet – nothing will destroy the quality of a herb quicker at this stage than exposure to light. Label the jars immediately with the name of the herb. Most domestic herb requirements are comparatively small; there is little point in storing them for posterity! It is better to keep just enough for the ensuing winter's needs.

At this stage, at the end of a busy week and a summer of cultivation, the amount of dried herb looks rather small and perhaps unrewarding. The finished product may weigh only an eighth of the original fresh weight, but nonetheless it retains all its aroma and essence.

Left:
A modest harvest of herbs drying in small bunches on the floor of a summer house. Warm spare rooms, garden shelters, barns – any space that is clean and dry can be used to dry household quantities of herbs.

Left:
Collect a few pretty sprigs of herbs and leaves in summer to press and preserve for winter gifts. Their beauty and aroma can be used to decorate cards, bookmarks and letter heads, and bring memories of summer herb gardens.

Rosemary for Remembrance

GIVE THIS DAINTY, HEART-SHAPED DECORATION TO YOUR VALENTINE OR HANG ONE ABOVE A BED OR A DRESSING-TABLE.

1 Although, traditionally red roses and rosebuds signify true love, we have broken with tradition and included some cream flowers to lighten the design a little and to give it variety.

3 Place two wheat stalks together. Cut another stalk into several short lengths and fasten these to the top of the two long stalks. They will form the top of the decoration. Bind short sprays of rosemary and the dried flowers along the length of the stalk, placing the rosebuds so that they face in opposite directions.

2 Twist the wire into a circle. Then, by pinching it at the base and the top, make it into a heart shape. Ours measured 8 inches in length. Cut short sprays of rosemary and bind two or three together on the frame with silver wire.

4 Tie the ribbon close to the top of the stalks so that it conceals the first stem binding. Fasten the stalk to the top and base of the heart and tuck in small flower sprays to conceal the wires. Wire a single rose to the side of the heart.

5 The rosemary will gradually dry on the decoration if it is hung in a warm, dry atmosphere. Then it will become a lasting token.

Midsummer Table Ring

CAPTURE THE ESSENCE OF SUMMER WITH THIS HIGHLY
SCENTED TABLE DECORATION. TO GIVE IT AN EXTRA
PZAZZ, YOU COULD REPLACE THE CLUSTER OF TAPERS
WITH SPARKLERS.

1 You can select herbs and flowers to match a specific
color scheme – lime green, yellow, and white, for
example, or go for a more random look and include flowers
in all the colors of the rainbow.

3 Add the bright daisy-like shapes of the feverfew, cutting
the stems short so that the lowest flowers lie close
against the foam. Add the caraway seedheads at intervals
around the ring.

2 Begin by concealing the foam ring beneath a layer of
herb leaves. We used individual scented geranium
leaves and small sprays of variegated mint to give the design
a light, bright look. Add small sprays of lady's mantle.

4 Cut short lengths from the base of some of the tapers
and arrange them in a group at one side of the ring.
Arrange the pinks in a cluster among them.

5 When the tapers are alight and flickering in a light
summer breeze, this will be a delightful table decoration
for a midsummer garden party.

Golden Flower Tree

THE GREAT THING ABOUT DESIGNING YOUR OWN TREES IS THAT YOU CAN STYLE THEM TO MATCH YOUR OWN FURNISHINGS, TO REMEMBER A SPECIAL OCCASION, SPECIAL MOMENT, OR TO BRING A SPLASH OF SUNSHINE INTO YOUR HOME. MODELING CLAY IS AVAILABLE IN MOST CRAFT STORES AND IN DEPARTMENT STORES.

1 You could use a plain earthenware flower pot, which would give the design a rustic look, but we chose one that had been painted with blue and then spattered with bright green, two colors that are repeated in the sprays of borage. Cover any drainage holes with masking tape.

3 Press the foam ball firmly on top of the twig. Cut short sprays of lady's mantle and arrange them all around the ball as the foundation of the design.

2 Shape the modeling clay into a ball, push the end of the twig into it and press the clay into the base of the flower pot. If necessary, use more clay to hold the twig in place.

4 Position sprays of bright yellow artemisia flowers and variegated mint all around the ball, then add color accents of blue borage at intervals. Trim off any unduly wayward ends.

5 Fill the flower pot with potpourri. Tie the ribbons around the twig just beneath the ball and cut the ends slantwise to neaten them. Spray the tree with a fine mist of water each day to keep the flowers fresh.

Herb Ball

WHETHER YOU WISH TO GIVE YOUR KITCHEN A
REFRESHING AROMA, TO KEEP INSECTS AT BAY, OR
SIMPLY TO STORE YOUR CULINARY HERBS IN AN
ATTRACTIVE WAY, THIS TRADITIONAL HERB BALL IS
THE IDEAL DECORATION.

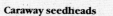

YOU WILL NEED

Half a stub wire

Floral foam ball soaked
in water; ours was
3 inches in diameter

String

Selection of herbs such
as rosemary, bay, sage,
purple sage, mint,
marjoram, and thyme

Caraway seedheads

Florists' scissors

Satin ribbon ½ inch
wide

Scissors

1 For a long-lasting decoration, make your choice from
the evergreen herbs — bay, rosemary, and sage — and
from spice seedheads such as caraway, fennel, and dill.

2 Bend the stub wire in half to make a staple and push it
into the foam ball. Hang the ball on a piece of string
while you work on the decoration. Cut the stems to almost
equal lengths — a perfectly round decoration would look
contrived — and build up the design by mixing the various
herbs all the way round.

3 Position the caraway seedheads, which are the
highlights of the decoration, more or less evenly around
the ball. Remove the string and hang the ball on a ribbon. Tie
a bow on top.

Dry Potpourri

TAKE A HANDFUL OF DRIED ROSE PETALS, LAVENDER, BAY LEAVES, AND ROSEMARY, ADD A SPRINKLING OF SPICES AND A FEW DROPS OF OIL OF ROSES AND YOU HAVE A ROMANTIC AND FRAGRANT POTPOURRI – IT REALLY IS AS SIMPLE AS IT SOUNDS.

1 You can vary the ingredients and the proportion of one to another to suit your own preferences or the materials that are available. Only the orris root powder, which acts as a fixative, has a practical role to play.

2 Mix the dried ingredients in a bowl with a spoon or, therapeutically, your fingers. Pour on a few drops of essential oil – oil of roses will give a sweet perfume, neroli a hint of orange-blossom freshness, and oil of lavender a note of nostalgia. Transfer the ingredients to a covered container and store it, away from direct light, for 6 weeks, stirring or shaking daily.

YOU WILL NEED

2 cups of dried rose petals

—

1 cup dried lavender

—

1 cup dried rosemary

—

A few bay leaves, crumbled

—

2 teaspoons grated nutmeg

—

1 tablespoon ground cinnamon

—

2 tablespoons orris root powder

—

3–4 drops oil of roses

—

Dried rosebud, to decorate

3 When all the scents are blended and the spices have lost their "rawness," the potpourri is ready to be displayed in your prettiest china, glass, or silver bowls, or in shells, jars, or baskets.

Scents of Proportion

THIS AROMATIC AND COLORFUL MEDLEY OF DRIED HERB LEAVES AND FLOWERS IS ARRANGED OVER BANDS OF LAVENDER FLOWERS AND POTPOURRI. IT'S A NOTION YOU CAN ADAPT TO ENHANCE SEE-THROUGH CONTAINERS OF ALL SHAPES AND SIZES.

1 The design is composed on a piece of dried foam, which is fixed into the center of the container and surrounded by lavender and potpourri. A small glass container could be fitted with a cylinder of foam; a large rectangular one may need a whole block. The jug shown in the photograph was fitted with a block standing on end and pared at the corners.

2 Cut the foam to fit the container, leaving a gap of about ½ inch all round. The foam should extend about 1 inch above the rim. Use adhesive clay to hold the plastic prong in the bottom of the container and press the shaped foam onto the prong. Spoon a layer of lavender flowers all around the foam, shaking the container to level it. Add a layer of potpourri, then spoon in more lavender flowers up to the rim.

3 Build up the outline of the arrangement with sprays of lady's mantle, positioning some stems so that they slant downwards over the rim. Position the lavender stems in groups of six or seven to achieve a massed effect.

4 Place the contrasting flowers between the fluffy outlines of the lady's mantle and spikes of lavender, with some rosebuds towards the back and a cluster close to the center, with one large feature rose – which was dried in a microwave – to one side.

5 Fill in the design with dried leaves and clusters of small
flowers to achieve a closely packed effect. Position one
feature flower, a rose or a peony, perhaps, close to the rim on
one side to give visual weight to the design.

Bridesmaid's Posy

THERE IS A LONG TRADITION IN MEDITERRANEAN COUNTRIES OF MOUNTING BRIDAL AND FIESTA POSIES ON BERIBBONED CANES. THIS DESIGN, WHICH IS AN INTERPRETATION OF THOSE STYLES, COULD BE CARRIED BY A YOUNG BRIDESMAID OR PAGEBOY AT A COUNTRY WEDDING.

1 Silver-leafed herbs such as sage, lavender, artemisia, and senecio look especially attractive with pastel-colored flowers in pink and blue. Variegated leaves — apple mint, golden thyme, and golden marjoram, for example — would look pretty with lemon, yellow, and orange flowers.

3 Arrange more flowers around the central feature. Alternate the flowers so that different shapes and colors are evenly distributed and include slender sprays of aromatic leaves to lighten the effect. Bind the stems with silver wire and trim the stem ends.

2 Bind the cane with white satin ribbon. Begin to compose the posy with a rose at the center, adding sage and artemisia in a ring around it. You can secure the first few stems at this stage by binding them with silver wire.

4 Cut a hole in the center of the mats and push them over the cane and the stems. Secure the mats in place with adhesive tape.

5 A floppy bow and long trails of pale blue ribbon – the ribbon illustrated here has a woven chequerboard pattern – complete a design that a small pageboy could carry. Spray the flowers with a fine mist of cool water and keep them in a cool place until just before the event.

YOU WILL NEED

Bunch of fresh lavender
—
Florists' scissors
—
Satin ribbon ½ inch wide
—
Scissors

Lavender Bottle

AS PRACTICAL AS IT IS PRETTY, THIS TRADITIONAL DECORATION CAN BE USED TO SCENT LINEN AND LINGERIE. IT COULD ALSO BE HUNG IN A CLOSET OR DISPLAYED IN A BASKET OF OLD LACE.

1 Lavender bottles get high marks for tradition, aroma, and usefulness but score indifferently in terms of color. Choose ribbon colors that will match or enhance the furnishings in your home or go for bright shades that will make an eye-catching group.

2 Select an uneven number of fresh, pliable lavender stems; we used 11. Group them together and tie the ribbon round the stems, just below the heads. Trim off one end of the ribbon, leaving the other trailing.

3 Carefully bend back the stalks just below the tie so that they enclose the flowerheads. Pull the long end of the ribbon through to the outside.

4 Weave the ribbon over one stalk, under the next, over the next and so on, round and round, and as far down the stems as you wish. Tie the ribbon neatly to secure it and cut off the excess. Tie a bow over the knot to conceal it and cut the ribbon ends slantwise. Cut the lavender stems level.

5 When the lavender stalks have been woven in and out with ribbons, the flowers are enclosed in a decorative cage and will not shed or drop and look messy among linen or lace.

Country Basket

IT MAY BE AN OLD BUT NOW DISCARDED FAVORITE OR ONE THAT YOU PICKED UP IN A CHARITY STORE, OR IT MAY JUST NOT FIT IN WITH YOUR CURRENT SCHEME OF THINGS — BUT HERE IS A WAY TO GIVE A NOT-SO-SPECIAL BASKET A COMPLETELY NEW LOOK.

1 You can use any dried herbs from your collection to make a fragrant mixture. Choose toning shades of paper ribbon to cover the herb and spice jars and to decorate the basket handle.

3 Working on a small area at a time, cover the basket sides with glue. Leave the glue to cool for a few seconds so that you do not burn your fingers, then press on handfuls of the hay and herb mixture. Surprisingly, the hay mixture will be so enmeshed and intertwined that it should stay in place.

2 Strip any leaves from the stalks and cut off the marjoram and lady's mantle flowers. Gently mix them with the hay, which we have used, or the moss, taking care not to crush the herbs.

4 Cut a length of paper ribbon and unfurl half of it. Tie it into a bow and fix it to the basket handle with half a stub wire threaded through the back of the loop. Cut the unfurled end slantwise to neaten it.

5 Form the fresh herbs and flowers into a posy, tie the stalks with raffia and cut the ends. Fill the basket with the kind of herb and spice goodies that a friend or relative would love to receive. We chose cinnamon cookies, caraway cookies, herbed vinegars, and a selection of dried spices in tiny jars.

YOU WILL NEED

Garlic, red and green chilies, cinnamon sticks, fresh ginger

—

Stub wires

—

Wire cutters

—

Selection of long-lasting herbs such as bay, rosemary, and purple sage

—

Florists' scissors

—

Roll of florists' silver wire

—

Raffia

Herb and Spice Posy

HERBS AND SPICES HAVE A DUAL ROLE TO PLAY IN THE KITCHEN: THEY ARE BOTH DECORATIVE AND USEFUL — ATTRACTIVE TO LOOK AT AND INVALUABLE FOR FLAVORINGS. THIS RAFFIA-TIED POSY PROVES THE POINT.

1 Even before you begin to arrange them, the components display their design potential. There is a strong color contrast between the garlic and the chilies, the glossy bay leaves and the matte surface of the purple sage.

2 Push a stub wire through one edge of a piece of fresh ginger and bend back the end of the wire to secure it.

3 Thread three chilies on to a stub wire so that they point in different directions and alternate the colors. Bend the end of the wire to form a hook and to hold the chilies in place.

4 Begin to arrange the posy in one hand. Gather together two or three stems of bay, which is the longest of the materials you will use, then add sprays of contrasting herbs. Push the stub wires securing the spices into the bunch of natural stems, where they will be concealed. Bind the stems securely with silver wire.

5 You can tie the stems with several strands of raffia, or with a raffia braid. Hang the finished arrangement in an alcove, in front of a mirror, in a window, or on the wall.

The Herb
Directory

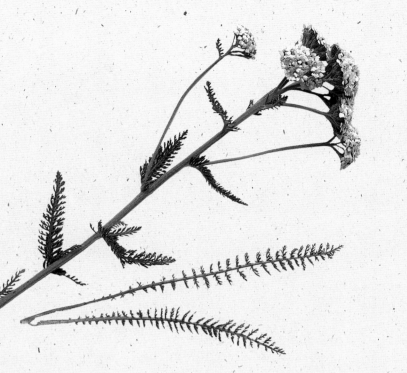

Achillea millefolium

YARROW

Above:

With its umbel-like clusters of minute white flowers and ladder-like leaves, yarrow is an attractive addition to a herbaceous border.

BUNCHES OF YARROW HANGING TO DRY IN A WARM AIRY ROOM; THE FLAT WHITE FLOWERHEADS PROVIDING HIGHLIGHTS IN A DRIED FLOWER ARRANGEMENT IN A SUMMER FIREPLACE; A FEW OF THE PUNGENT LEAVES ADDED SPARINGLY TO A MIXED GREEN SALAD . . .

Common yarrow, a hardy perennial and native to Europe, grows as a rampant weed in fields and hedges, where it can vary from a low, creeping form to a tough plant up to 24 inches high. It has flat heads of minute five-petalled white flowers. Other forms (*A. millefolium v. rosea* and *A. filipendulina,* respectively) have pink-and-cream or bright yellow flowers.

HISTORY

The plant's generic name is believed to derive from the Greek hero Achilles, who is said to have used it to heal his soldiers' wounds during the Trojan War. Accordingly, it has been called *herba militaris,* the military herb, knight's milfoil, bloodwort, and staunchweed.

IDENTIFICATION

The leaves are about 4 inches long, dark green, downy, and feathery, and the stems are pale green, rough, and angular. The plant flowers from early summer to late fall.

KEY TO SYMBOLS

	Culinary
	Healing
	Cosmetics
	Scented
	Decorative
	Warning

CULTIVATION

Propagate from seed or root divison. Specialist seedsmen offer seed for spring sowing and seedlings may be dotted about the herb border as yarrow has a reputation for improving the condition of plants in its vicinity. From seed the plants may prove slow to establish, taking a year or two to develop (even in dry warm regions) as the plants are drought-tolerant.

HOW TO USE

Fresh leaves may be used in salads. They have a slightly pungent taste and are very aromatic.

In self-help medicine, fresh leaves were applied to wounds as an aid to healing. An infusion of fresh or dried leaves may be used to apply to minor cuts and grazes, and a decoction may be used to wash the hair; it was thought to prevent baldness. It can also be helpful as an astringent for greasy skin.

Left:

In its natural habitat, yarrow stands out like so many snowflakes against the grassy background.

Allium sativum

GARLIC

GOLDEN GARLIC-FRIED CROUTONS GARNISHING A
CREAMY VEGETABLE SOUP; A CLOVE OF GARLIC
RUBBED AROUND A SALAD BOWL TO IMPART JUST A
HINT OF THE FLAVOR; SLIVERS OF THE BULB TUCKED
INTO SLITS OF LAMB FOR GRILLING OR ROASTING. . .

A member of the onion family, the garlic bulb is an indispensable flavoring in cooking and is widely used throughout
southern Europe, the Middle East, the Far East, Africa, the
West Indies, Mexico, and North and South America. A native of
Asia, it is easily grown and widely cultivated in warm climates
throughout the world. It can be grown successfully in northern
Europe and in North America, but in cooler conditions the
bulb never reaches its maximum flavor potential.

HISTORY

Garlic has been used medicinally and as a flavoring for at least
5,000 years, and has been cultivated in the Mediterranean
region since the time of the ancient Egyptians. The Anglo-
Saxons grew it, too, and gave it its name: *gar*, a lance, and *leac*,
a leek. Roman soldiers ate it as a stimulant, and ancient
mariners always took it as a part of their ships' stores.

IDENTIFICATION

The straight, rigid stem, topped by a spherical pink or white
flowerhead, grows to a height of 2 feet. Each bulb is made up
of several cloves, which may have white, pink, or purple skin,
encased in a paper-like sheath.

The size, number, and flavor of the cloves vary considerably according to the variety and the climate. Indeed, garlic
may be highly pungent or almost sweet. The bright green
leaves are long, straight, slender, and round, similar to those
of chives.

Below:
*Cloves of garlic wrapped in
their papery sheaths and
broken away from the bulb
represent untold depths of
flavor packed into such
small and insignificant-
looking units.*

CULTIVATION

Garlic grows best in well-drained soil in a sunny position. Cloves are planted in the fall or in early spring to mature in summer. They should be planted 1 inch deep and up to 8 inches apart, and should be given a good start with the application of a general fertilizer.

It is said that if garlic is planted beneath a peach tree it will prevent leaf-curl, and that it can ward off aphids and blackspot on roses.

HOW TO USE

Garlic cloves may be finely chopped or crushed with a garlic press and used to complement the flavor of meat, fish, vegetables, salad dressings, sauces, and egg dishes. The more finely it is chopped the stronger its flavor. In southern Europe, sauces such as *aioli* (garlic mayonnaise) and *skordalia* are made from raw garlic, and in one French dish chicken is cooked surrounded by whole cloves of garlic and salt. Some people may find the aftertaste of garlic offensive on the breath. Try chewing fennel seeds after eating to alleviate this problem.

Whole cloves, peeled, may be preserved in jars filled with olive oil; the flavored oil may then be used to add a piquant taste to a salad dressing.

Garlic has positive health-giving properties. It may be used as an antiseptic; to tone up the digestive system; to reduce blood pressure; and to clear catarrh and bronchitis. It has also been used as a diuretic and as a combatant to diseases such as typhoid.

GARLIC MASHED POTATOES

Serves 6

Ingredients

3 heads of garlic (about 35 cloves)
½ cup butter
¼ cup flour
¼ teaspoon nutmeg
¼ teaspoon English mustard
1 cup boiling milk
salt and pepper
2 pounds floury potatoes
3 tablespoons light cream

Garlic Mashed Potatoes are particularly good with sausages, steak, and roast chicken, or as a nest for baked eggs.

Preparation

Separate the garlic cloves and blanch them in boiling water for 1 minute; drain and peel. Then cook over a low heat, covered, in half the butter for about 20 minutes until tender.

—

Blend in the flour, nutmeg, and mustard, and stir for several minutes without browning. Remove from the heat and stir in the boiling milk. Season with salt and pepper to taste.

—

Return to the heat and simmer for 5 minutes. Sieve or blend to a smooth purée. Return to the pan and simmer for 2 more minutes.

—

Peel the potatoes and cut into small chunks. Boil for 15 minutes or until just tender and drain. Mash with the remaining butter.

—

Beat in the reheated garlic purée followed by the cream, a spoonful at a time. The final mixture should not be too runny. Check for seasoning and serve immediately.

Left:
A single ram-rod straight stem of flowering chives and two round, hollow leaves illustrate the statuesque nature of the plant.

Below:
A thick cluster of chives topped by their pinky-purple flower dome is one of the prettiest and most colorful features of an herb garden.

Allium schoenoprasum

CHIVES

SNIPPED CHIVES MINGLING WITH SOUR CREAM IN A DRESSING FOR BAKED POTATOES; CHIVE LEAVES AND CARROT "FLOWERS" MAKING A DECORATIVE GARNISH ON A VEGETABLE PATE; PATS OF CHIVE BUTTER DRIZZLING OVER CHARCOAL-GRILLED STEAKS...

Chives, a member of the onion family and grown from bulbs, are native to northern Europe, where they may sometimes be found growing wild. They also thrive in temperate regions of North America. The leaves have a delicate, onion-like flavor and are widely used in cooking, particularly in egg and cheese dishes, in salads, and as a garnish. If protected under a cloche, they can be harvested for nine months of the year. Chives are included in the *fines herbes* mixture used in French cookery.

HISTORY
In the Middle Ages, chives were known as "rush-leek", from the Greek *schoinos*, rush, and *prason*, a leek. They have been cultivated since the sixteenth century.

IDENTIFICATION
Chives grow in clumps, with their round, hollow, grass-like leaves reaching a height of 9 inches. Some varieties, *A. sibiricum* for example, may be 15 inches tall. The stems are firm, straight, smooth and, like the leaves, bright dark green. The flowers, which bloom for two months in midsummer, form round deep-purple or pink heads and make an attractive garnish.

CULTIVATION

Divide established clumps of bulbs every three years in the spring, and transplant clusters from the outer edges of the clumps. Alternatively, chives can be raised afresh from seed. Although they thrive in any good garden loam, they show a marked preference for slightly acid soil and need to be kept moist throughout the growing season. Choose a place where they can enjoy some shade during the day and remove the flower heads to maintain a continuous supply of flavorsome leaves. The foliage dies down in the winter, so cover a plant or two with dry leaves to encourage a few early spikes for their fresh flavor. Alternatively, plant a clump of bulbs in the fall to keep in a porch or on the apartment window-sill for fresh early spikes. In those regions where the summer temperature remains above 90° clumps can be planted out afresh in the fall to provide a winter supply of leaves.

In the garden allow at least two or three plants to flower for the sheer beauty of the purple-pink bobbed heads. Float these as a garnish in soups – especially consommé – or use them to decorate the cheese board or cold collations.

HOW TO USE

Snipped chives – for it is easier to cut them with scissors than chop them with a knife – give a hint of onion flavor in many dishes, from scrambled egg to cheese soufflé. They are good sprinkled on green and tomato salads, on soups, in cream cheese sandwiches, and on baked potatoes with sour cream dressing. Chive butter, made by beating snipped chives and lemon juice into softened butter, is good with grilled chops and steak.

The leaves are slightly antiseptic, and in addition were used to relieve rheumatism.

LIME-CHIVE BUTTER LOG

Ingredients

1 cup lightly salted or sweet butter, softened
7 tablespoons snipped fresh chives
2 tablespoons frozen lime juice concentrate, thawed
1 tablespoon chopped fresh thyme or ½ teaspoon ground thyme

Use to sauté veal or pork chops and drizzle over seafood or fish.

Preparation

When the butter has reached room temperature, beat all the ingredients together in a small bowl.

—

Transfer the mixture in the shape of a 12 inch log onto a piece of freezer paper or plastic wrap and roll up, twisting the ends of the paper to seal.

—

Refrigerate until firm or freeze.

—

Each log yields about a dozen 1 teaspoon pats of butter.

Aloysia triphylla

LEMON VERBENA

BAKED TROUT MADE ALL THE MORE AROMATIC WITH A
LEMON VERBENA STUFFING; PEARS POACHED IN A
SYRUP FLAVORED WITH THE LEMONY HERB; A GREEN
AND GOLD POTPOURRI BLENDED WITH THE SHARP,
TANGY, FRAGRANCE OF THE LEAVES. . .

One of the most delightful of scented plants, lemon verbena
has a strong citrus aroma that is at its most powerful in the
early evening. A native of South America, it thrives best in hot
climates, where it will grow up to 5 feet tall and almost as
wide. It is, therefore, a good choice as a back-of-the-bed plant
in sunny borders.

HISTORY
The plant was brought to Europe by the Spaniards, and was
used as a source of fragrant oil for perfume.

IDENTIFICATION
The woody stems are tough, angular, and have many branches,
giving the plant, which grows to a height of 5 feet, its bushy,
spreading characteristic. The long, pointed oval, and pale
green leaves are about 4 inches long and ½ inch wide. The
flowers, which grow in clusters along the stem, are pale purple
and bloom in late summer.

CULTIVATION
A perennial, deciduous shrub, lemon verbena is hardy to a
temperature of 40°. This means that in cool climates it needs
protection in winter. It may be grown from seed, or from soft
cuttings taken in summer and grown in sandy soil under
cover. The bush should be pruned in spring to contain its
growth and remove dead wood.

HOW TO USE
The strong citrus aroma is used to flavor stuffings for meat,
poultry, and fish, in fish dishes and sauces, fruit salads, poached
fruit, soft drinks, and cream candies. The herb may be substi-
tuted for lemongrass in south-east Asian dishes.

Fresh or dried leaves may be used medicinally, as a mild
sedative, and as a help for indigestion and flatulence, or may
be infused to make a mild skin toner and skin freshener.

The dried leaves are an invaluable ingredient in potpourri,
particularly when used to scent bed linen or in a herbal sleep
pillow.

Above:

*The long, pointed oval
leaves of lemon verbena
are packed with a subtle
citrus-like aroma.*

Left:

*Towering high above other
herbs and flowering plants,
lemon verbena makes a
striking impact in any herb
garden.*

Right:

With its pale sugar-almond pink flowers and downy leaves, English mallow is attractive enough to use in summer flower arrangements.

Althaea officinalis

ENGLISH MALLOW

THE YOUNG, BRIGHT GREEN SHOOTS SHREDDED AND ADDED TO MIXED SALADS, OR CHOPPED OVER AVOCADO SALAD; THE ROOTS, LIGHTLY BOILED, FRIED IN SIZZLING BUTTER AND GARNISHED WITH CHOPPED CORIANDER. . .

Below:

In the damp conditions that it favors English mallow will grow to a height of 4 feet.

A member of the hollyhock family, English mallow has small but attractive flowers carried without stems. It is grown throughout Europe, in Australia, Asia, and eastern North America. The mucilage, which comprises about 30 per cent of the roots, stems, and leaves, was used to make the confection known as marshmallow, but now substitutes are used commercially.

HISTORY

The plant's medicinal properties have been recognized since ancient times. English mallow features in a 2nd-century BC herbal, and was illustrated in another from the 6th century AD.

IDENTIFICATION

The plant grows to a height of up to 4 feet, with a spread of 18 inches. The long, tapering root is cream colored and fleshy, somewhat resembling a parsnip, and the bright green leaves are heart-shaped and irregularly toothed, with pronounced veins in a yellowish green and a downy coating on both sides. The five-petaled flowers are saucer-shaped, white, or pink, and about 1½ inches across. They bloom in late summer. The plant has no fragrance.

CULTIVATION

Althaea officinalis is a European native of brackish marshes and therefore appreciates dampish soils. It is propagated by root division in fall or early winter, and rarely from seed. Cut back the top growth each fall to encourage good lush shoots the following year.

On the other hand, the garden hollyhock is propagated from fresh seed sown in the late summer to flower 18 months later. Alternatively, when it is sown in boxes or pots in the spring, rosettes are formed in the first summer and the growing spike the second. Plant out at the back of the border or against the shelter of a hedge or a wall where the swaying upright spikes can be shown off to advantage.

HOW TO USE

The young leaves and shoots may be shredded and added to salads and soups; the roots may be parboiled, then fried in butter.

The plant was used in self-help medicine for sprains, bruises, and muscular pain. An infusion of the dried root was used to treat sore throats and ulcers, while an infusion of flowers was used as a mouthwash.

Anethum graveolens

DILL

FRESH DILL LEAVES — KNOWN AS DILL WEED — IN A
SAUCE TO SERVE WITH OVEN-BAKED BREAM; CHOPPED
DILL STIRRED INTO YOGURT AS A DRESSING FOR
CUCUMBER; DILL SEED AS A PICKLING SPICE FOR
PICKLES. . .

The plant originates from southern Europe and western Asia,
and its use is recorded far back in time. As with so many
umbellifers, this hardy annual yields two separate culinary
components, its seeds and its feathery leaves, which are,
somewhat ambiguously, known as dill weed.

HISTORY

The herb was used medicinally by doctors in both ancient
Egypt and Rome; indeed, it was the Romans who introduced it
to northern Europe. After centuries in obscurity, it surfaced
again in medieval times, when its use was widespread, particularly in Scandinavian countries like Norway and Sweden.

IDENTIFICATION

Dill grows to a height of 2½ feet, with a spread of 12 inches.
The green stem, which is hollow and smooth, branches out at
the top and carries large flat umbellifers of bright yellow
flowers that bloom in midsummer. The leaves are ultra-fine,
feathery, and dark green, and have a taste similar to that of
parsley. The flat, oval seeds are parchment colored, and have
a rather bitter flavor.

CULTIVATION

Sow seeds in a sunny spot, then thin the seedlings out so that
they are about 8 inches apart. They resent being transplanted,
and show their displeasure by bolting into flower prematurely.
Sow in the spring as soon as the ground is warm, and follow
with small sowings at 2 week intervals throughout the summer
to maintain a good supply of fresh leaves. Where winters are
very mild, seed can be sown in the fall to overwinter and
provide a good early crop the following spring, or self-sown
seedlings will overwinter. Never sow near to fennel, as the
two plants tend to cross and the subsequent seed is not as
flavorsome as might be expected. The filmy foliage may be cut
about six weeks after sowing and the seed collected when
fully ripe.

Above:

*Dill leaves, soft, feathery
and densely packed, are
perfect candidates for
drying, when they are
known as dill weed.*

HOW TO USE

The fresh leaves are used in salads, fish dishes, and sauces to
serve with fish. In Germany and eastern Europe it is used in
pickles, as a preservative for sour cabbage (sauerkraut) and
small cucumbers, known as dill pickles.

The seeds produce an oil that is used to make dill water, or
gripe water, used to alleviate colic in babies. The seeds are
also said to act as a sedative and to ward off hunger.

Overleaf:

*The star-like clusters of
yellowish-green flowers
carried on long stems make
dill a dramatic plant,
especially in the sunlight.*

SOUSED HERRINGS WITH SOUR CREAM

Serves 6

Ingredients

6 fresh herring fillets
1 large Spanish onion, sliced
6 bay leaves
18 whole black peppercorns
1 cup red wine vinegar mixed with water
1 cup sour cream
fresh dill, chopped

Oven temperature: 325°

Preparation

Preheat the oven. Wash the herring fillets and pat them dry with paper towels.

—

Place some of the thinly sliced onion, a bay leaf, and 3 whole peppercorns on each fish. Roll up the herrings with the tail-end away from you. Place in an ovenproof dish and cover with the vinegar and water mixture.

—

Place in a moderate oven until the herrings are cooked — about 20 minutes. Let the fish cool in the liquid for several hours or overnight.

—

Serve cold with a spoonful of sour cream garnished with chopped dill.

Angelica archangelica

ANGELICA

CHOPPED ANGELICA LEAVES IN A *COURT BOUILLON* FOR SALMON AND TROUT; YOUNG SHOOTS AS A FLAVORING FOR RHUBARB COMPOTE; CANDIED SHOOTS AS A SWEETMEAT AND DECORATION FOR CAKES AND DESSERTS. . .

A giant member of the parsley family, angelica grows up to 5 feet, with a spread of about 3 feet. It is native both to northern Europe and to Syria, and grows wild in many parts of the world, decorating the countryside with its bright green shoots of tree-like proportions.

HISTORY
In ancient times the plant was believed to ward off evil spirits, and was used at pagan festivals. Its later association with angels, in its botanical name and in many European languages, is thought to derive from the fact that it came into flower on or around 8 May, the feast day of St Michael the Archangel.

IDENTIFICATION
The whole plant is pleasantly aromatic. It has large fleshy roots that can weigh up to 3 pounds and thick, sturdy, and hollow stems that are purple at the base, shading to bright and light green. The plant reaches a height of 5 feet and the huge leaves, made up of three leaflets, are bright green and finely toothed. The flowers, which appear in mid- to late summer, are small and yellowish green in color, forming umbrella-like clusters.

CULTIVATION
Angelica seed loses its viability so it is important to sow the seed when fresh. If this cannot be done, store it in a refrigerator or ice box throughout the winter, and then sow in the spring in tiny pinches, thinning out all but the best plants once germination has taken place. The seedlings do not transplant well, but it is worth trying when they are very small. Plant out at least 3 feet apart to allow the plants to develop uninhibited.

A good rich loam ensures the most marvellous of all herb garden plants, otherwise growth will be restricted and poor in color. Angelica dislikes hot, humid climates and appreciates a spot in gardens where it can be in the shade for some part of every day.

HOW TO USE
The fleshy stems are candied as cake decorations and sweetmeat. Young shoots may be blanched, chopped, and added to salads, and the leaves used to flavor *court bouillon* for fish, stewed fruits (rhubarb, in particular,) and preserves. Oil from the seeds is used as a flavoring in several aperitifs and other alcoholic drinks, including absinthe and gin. It is also used as an aromatic ingredient in potpourri.

Medicinally, the dried roots may be used as an aid to flatulence, and the leaves, shoots, and seeds to help relieve coughs, colds, and other respiratory disorders. The seeds may also be used as an appetite stimulant and an aid to digestion.

Above:
Clusters of angelica seedheads, and large fleshy leaves carried on stems which, when candied, make a delicious sweetmeat.

Left:
Silhouetted against a background of low-growing herbs, angelica is one of the most "architectural" plants in the herb garden.

Anthemis n.obilis

CHAMOMILE

CHAMOMILE TEA AS A SOOTHING DRINK FOR PETER
RABBIT AND OTHERS WITH NERVOUS EXCITEMENT OR
STOMACH AILMENTS; A SPRING, DAISY-FLOWERED
CHAMOMILE LAWN. . .

Apple-scented chamomile, a perennial plant of the composite
family, is one of the daintiest of herbs. A low-growing type
known as Roman chamomile can be grown as an effective
ground cover to form a green and white daisy-flowered lawn.

HISTORY
It is said that the ancient Egyptians used chamomile as a cure
for ague. Its use was widespread in the Middle Ages, not only
in southern Europe, where it originates, but throughout
northern Europe, too. It is mentioned as a medicinal herb in
both John Gerard's and Nicholas Culpeper's herbals.

IDENTIFICATION
The plant may grow to a height of 12 inches. It has shallow,
fibrous roots and a green, hairy, branching stem. The leaves
are finely cut and feathery, and the flowers, which come in
summer, are creamy white with yellow conical centers.

CULTIVATION
The plant is easily grown from the division of runners, which
are planted out in early spring, and from seed; it is also a
prolific self-seeder. It prefers a fertile, moist soil in a sunny
position, but will cling tenaciously to life in a poor, well-
drained soil. There is a non-flowering variety, "Treneague,"
which some people prefer to use for lawns.

Above, right:
Shaggy stems of
chamomile, with their
small, insignificant leaves,
are topped by delicate,
daisy-like cream flowers.

Right:
A dense patch of
chamomile is seen growing
among other herbs, the
dainty flowers all turned to
face the sun.

HOW TO USE
What the plant lacks in culinary uses – there are none – it
makes up for in other ways. A tisane of the flowers is taken for
dyspepsia, flatulence, and other stomach ailments, and used
as a mild antiseptic. It can also be taken as an appetite restorer.

An infusion of the dried flowers is used as a rinse for fair
hair, as a skin cleanser, and a skin tonic. One species, *A.
tinctoria*, is used as an orange-brown dye.

CHAMOMILE CLEANSING MILK

*As this lotion is based on milk, it must be kept in a cool place and will
not last for more than 2 or 3 days. It is excellent for oily skins.*

Ingredients
3 tablespoons chamomile flowers
1 cup warm milk

Preparation
Leave the flowers to infuse in the warm milk until the milk
smells strongly of chamomile. As it is important that a skin
should not form on the milk, and essential that the milk should
not be allowed to boil, the best way of keeping the infusion
warm is to use a bowl placed over a saucepan of hot water off
the heat.

—

Stir the milk gently from time to time so as not to break up the
flowers.

—

Strain the scented milk into a screw-topped bottle or jar.

Anthriscus cerefolium 🏛 👁

CHERVIL

TINY SPRIGS OF GARDEN-FRESH CHERVIL ADDED TO
BECHAMEL SAUCE AS AN ACCOMPANIMENT TO FISH;
THE CURLED AND LACY LEAVES USED AS A GARNISH FOR
CHEESE OR CHICKEN DISHES; THE CHOPPED FRESH
LEAVES ADDED TO A FLUFFY OMELET ON THE POINT OF
SERVING. . .

Chervil, together with chives, parsley, and tarragon, is one of
the *fines herbes* mixture used in French cookery, particularly
to flavor omelets. It is also one of the herbs used in *ravigote*
sauces, and is often blended with tarragon to flavor béchamel
and other creamy sauces. It is a hardy annual, one that is easy
to grow but that quickly goes to seed.

Above:

*Chervil, with its fern-like
leaves, is one of the fines
herbes mixture widely
used in French cookery.*

HISTORY

The plant is a native of the Middle East, southern Russia, and
the Caucasus, and was almost certainly introduced to
northern Europe by the Romans. It became one of the classic
herbs used in French cookery, in which it is considered
indispensable.

IDENTIFICATION

A member of the umbellifer family, chervil is closely related
to parsley. It grows to a height of 20 inches, with a spread of
about 8 inches. It has flat, light green and lacy leaves, which
have a slightly aniseed-like aroma and turn reddish brown as
the plant matures. It blooms in mid-summer, producing flat
umbellifers of tiny white flowers.

CULTIVATION

The plant can be easily grown from seed planted in early
spring or late summer in the position where it is to grow; a
trough or a window-box is ideal. A succession of sowings will
produce a harvest well into the winter. It likes a moist, shady
position, and should be kept well watered.

HOW TO USE

The leaves quickly lose their flavor and are best added fresh
to a dish just before serving. They can be chopped into
softened butter to serve with grilled meats or poultry; added
as an aromatic garnish to creamy soups, and stirred into egg
and cheese dishes. The leaves are also used to flavor white
wine vinegar, and may be infused in water as a skin freshener.

ROAST RIB OF BEEF WITH
BEARNAISE SAUCE

Serves 6

Ingredients

4 pounds beef rib
sea salt and freshly ground black pepper
½ cup sweet butter

For the Bearnaise sauce
1 cup sweet butter, cut into cubes
4 shallots, finely chopped
3 tablespoons white wine vinegar
2 tablespoons fresh tarragon, chopped
½ teaspoon chopped chervil
pinch of ground black pepper and salt
4 egg yolks
2 tablespoons cold water

Oven temperature: 425°

Preparation

Season the rib of beef with salt and pepper, and place in a heavy roasting pan. Melt the butter and cook in a hot oven, browning the meat on both sides. For rare meat, cook for 10 minutes per pound on each side. Remove the meat to a serving plate and keep warm.

—

To make the sauce, in a small heavy saucepan melt 1 tablespoon butter. Add the shallots. Cook slowly for about 10 minutes, then add the vinegar, half the tarragon and chervil, and salt and pepper to taste. Reduce the sauce to about 2 teaspoons.

—

Cool the mixture and add the egg yolks and cold water. Mix with a whisk over a low heat, or in a double boiler or saucepan. Make sure you amalgamate the eggs with the shallot mixture, but do not cook them or the sauce will be ruined.

—

When the egg yolks look thick and creamy, gradually whisk the remaining butter in, making sure the sauce does not separate. If it gets too thick, add a little water.

—

When the sauce is finished, add more chopped tarragon and chervil. Keep warm in the double boiler or double saucepan.

—

Carve the rib of beef and serve the Bearnaise sauce separately.

Armoracia rusticana

HORSERADISH

THE EYE-TINGLING PUNGENCY OF THE GROUND ROOT
TAMED BY BLENDING WITH CREAM OR YOGURT AS A
SAUCE FOR ROAST BEEF; THE GRATED ROOT ADDED
CAUTIOUSLY TO A STUFFING FOR TROUT; THE SAUCE
STIRRED INTO PIPED MASHED POTATO TO GIVE IT AN
UNMISTAKEABLE "BITE" . . .

Horseradish sauce, the classic British accompaniment to roast
beef, presents this herb at its most pungent, and in its most
popular form. The large fleshy roots are strongly aromatic, so
much so that they can, like raw onions, make your eyes water
as you prepare them. Unusually, for a herb, the large coarse
leaves have no aroma and no known uses.

Left:
Horseradish leaves, which
have no aroma and are not
used in cooking, are dark
green, thick and sword-like.

Right:
Horseradish with its tough
dark-green leaves and
penetrating roots will grow
in the most inhospitable of
places and is often found
along the wayside.

67

HISTORY

A native of northern Europe, and still found growing wild along roadsides in Britain and North America, horseradish has been used as a flavoring for at least 3,000 years. It was known to the ancient Greeks, and was used in Britain before the time of the Romans. During the Middle Ages, it was used in Germany and Denmark as a condiment, an alternative to mustard.

IDENTIFICATION

This perennial plant has long, thick, fleshy white roots covered by a rough and hairy brown skin. The leaves, which can be up to 20 inches long, are deep green and strongly marked with yellow veins. The stem, about 2 feet high, carries spikes of tiny white flowers in late spring and early summer.

CULTIVATION

Horseradish is an avid coloniser of whatever space is available, so restraint is necessary. It is grown by dividing and replanting the root; a piece about 8 inches long is ideal. It likes a deep, moist soil but will thrive anywhere. To harvest, dig up a piece of the root, and wash, and scrape it under water to prevent eye irritation.

HOW TO USE

A food processor is ideal for grating the peeled root. You can store it in vinegar or oil in a screw-topped jar, mix it with cream, sour cream, yogurt, mayonnaise, or cream cheese and dressings for sauces to serve with meat, fish, and potatoes. It is especially good with beef and smoked trout.

POTATO SALAD WITH HORSERADISH

Serves 4

Ingredients

1½ pounds new potatoes
½ cup sour cream
3 tablespoons horseradish, finely grated
pinch of paprika
½ teaspoon honey
salt and freshly ground black pepper
bunch of scallions or chives
handful of chopped parsley

Preparation

Wash the potatoes, but do not peel. Boil in salted water until tender.

—

Meanwhile, make the dressing. Combine the sour cream with the horseradish, paprika, and honey. Mix well and season with salt and pepper.

—

Trim the scallions and slit down the stalks so they curl outwards; or chop the chives.

—

When the potatoes are cooked, slice them while still hot and mix into the dressing with the parsley. Garnish with the onions or chives. Serve immediately, or chill and serve cold.

IDENTIFICATION

The plant can grow to a height of 3 feet with a spread of 2 feet. The woody stem has many soft, branching shoots covered with strong, feathery, grey-green leaves. The tiny flowers, which appear in late summer, are golden yellow.

CULTIVATION

Southernwood appreciates a well drained soil enriched with some leaf mold or compost, and needs to be protected from strong winds. Take cuttings of the new growth in early summer, or hard wood cuttings with a heel in fall. Leave all the growth on through the winter in spite of its bedraggled appearance (which has earned it the colloquial name of old man) as this growth will protect the woody stems from the effect of cold winds. Cut back in early spring to produce lush fresh growth. Only hardy in more temperate regions.

HOW TO USE

The pungent leaves of southernwood were used in Italy as a flavoring for meat and poultry stuffings, and for cakes, but they have few culinary uses now.

Medicinally, the dried plant may be used as an antiseptic and a stimulant. An infusion of the leaves may be used as a hair rinse to combat dandruff.

Dried leaves can be used in linen bags to repel insects, and also in potpourri.

A yellow dye can be extracted from the stems.

Left:
Southernwood leaves are strong, feathery, and deep grey-green in color. They have a pungent aroma.

Artemisia abrotanum

SOUTHERNWOOD

BUNCHES OF SOUTHERNWOOD HANGING IN CLOTHES CLOSETS TO WARD OFF MOTHS AND OTHER INSECTS; THE DRIED LEAVES LIGHTLY CRUMBLED IN POTPOURRI OR BLENDED WITH OTHER DRIED MATERIALS IN LINEN SACHETS . . .

With the delightful popular names of lad's love and old man, southernwood, a busy shrub, is grown in many cottage gardens and herbaceous borders as a decorative and strongly aromatic plant, which is, however, said to be repellant to bees. The French called it *garde-robe* because they used it in wardrobes to ward off moths.

HISTORY

Dioscorides described the plant as having such fine leaves that it seemed to be "furnished with hair," while in his herbal, Culpeper attributes it with the power of curing baldness. He recommended rubbing a paste made of the ashes and salad oil on the head or face to promote hair growth.

Left:
A dense patch of southernwood looks so tactile, one longs to bury a hand deep among the fragrant leaves.

Artemisia dracunculus.

TARRAGON

A BOTTLE OF GLOWING-GOLDEN TARRAGON VINEGAR TO USE IN PIQUANT SALAD DRESSINGS; FRESH LEAVES CHOPPED INTO CLASSIC BEARNAISE SAUCE OR THE DELICATELY FLAVORED *POULET A L'ESTRAGON;* LIGHT-AS-A-FEATHER OMELETS FLAVORED WITH *FINES HERBES . . .*

A distinction must be made between the true French tarragon or estragon and its Russian counterpart, *A. dracunculoides*, which is much coarser, and has paler leaves and a bitter taste. Contrarily, the latter is easier to grow!

French tarragon has a subtle flavor and is one of the four ingredients of the *fines herbes* mixture. It is one of the great culinary herbs of France, and has a battery of dishes created around it – *poulet à l'éstragon* and *oeufs en gelée à l'éstragon*, to name just two.

Above:

The leaves of the true French tarragon are long, slender, pointed and a rich dark green.

HISTORY

The plant, a hardy perennial, originates from southern Europe. The reference in its name to a "little dragon" is thought to derive from its folkloric reputation of curing the bites of snakes, serpents, and the like.

IDENTIFICATION

The plant grows to a height of 3 feet, with a spread of up to 18 inches. The leaves are dark green, long, slender, and pointed, about 3 inches long towards the base of the plant and considerably smaller at the tip of the stems. The flowers are lime green and formed in loose clusters. But the plant neither flowers nor sets seed in a cool climate.

CULTIVATION

A plant for the sunniest driest places, tarragon is a lover of warmth and good drainage. The top growth needs to be cut back early in the fall. In colder parts it needs to be protected in some way to help it through the winter. Dry bracken or leaves or a peat mulch covered with plastic is usually sufficient, but in more extreme conditions apply the mulch after the ground has frozen solid, using dry straw or salt hay.

You can also try to pot up a young plant to grow inside and keep through the winter. It will need a place where it gets whatever sunshine is available. Tarragon is not easy to keep in this way, so do not be too disheartened if it decides to go – nothing will persuade it to remain! Propagation is from root divison or stem cuttings – seed offered is usually that of Russian tarragon.

HOW TO USE

Tarragon has a strong and distinctive flavor, and must be used sparingly, especially as it is usually associated with delicate dishes such as chicken, white fish, creamy sauces, and egg and cheese recipes. Fresh sprigs of the herb are used to flavor vinegar for use in salad dressings and sauces.

ORANGE & TARRAGON CHICKEN

Serves 4

I n g r e d i e n t s

2 tablespoons butter
2 tablespoons vegetable oil
4 boneless chicken breasts, each weighing approx. 6 ounces
1 large onion, finely chopped
1 cup frozen concentrated orange juice
½ cup chicken stock
4 sprigs fresh tarragon or 1 tablespoon dried tarragon
1 tablespoon cornstarch
½ cup sour cream

P r e p a r a t i o n

Heat the butter and oil in a flameproof casserole. Brown the chicken thoroughly on all sides. Put to one side and remove and discard the skin.

—

Cook the onion in the casserole for 2–3 minutes. Stir in the orange juice, stock, and chopped tarragon. Bring to the boil and return chicken to the casserole. Cover and reduce the heat to a gentle simmer. Cook for 1 hour or until the chicken is tender.

—

Blend the cornstarch with 2 tablespoons water and stir into the casserole. Bring to the boil, stirring, until the sauce is smooth and thickened. Switch off the heat and stir in the sour cream. Leave to warm through for a few minutes.

—

Transfer the chicken breasts onto individual hot dinner plates. Spoon the sauce over the chicken.

CUCUMBER & AVOCADO WITH BORAGE

Serves 4

Ingredients

2 large cucumbers, about 2 pounds total weight
1 small avocado
lemon juice
¼ cup sweet butter
1 shallot, finely chopped
1 small egg, beaten
salt and freshly ground white pepper
2 tablespoons cream cheese, chopped
flowers from 2–3 sprigs borage

Preparation

Peel the cucumbers and cut each one into 4 equal lengths. Cut out a V-shaped wedge, about a quarter of the diameter of the cucumber, along the length of each piece and scoop out and discard the seeds. Chop the remaining wedges roughly.

—

Steam the cucumber lengths for about 12–15 minutes until just tender. Meanwhile, peel, halve, and remove the pit from the avocado. Cut off 8 slices, brush with lemon juice, and reserve for the garnish. Chop the remaining flesh roughly.

—

Heat the butter, add the chopped cucumber and shallot, and cook over a moderate heat for 4–5 minutes, stirring occasionally. Remove from the heat and stir in the avocado, egg, and seasoning so the egg scrambles very lightly. Scatter the cheese over, fold through once then pile the mixture into the cucumber lengths and scatter the borage over the top.

—

Serve the filled cucumber immediately with the reserved avocado slices.

Borago officinalis

BORAGE

DAINTY BLUE BORAGE FLOWERS AND YOUNG SHOOTS FLOATING IN ICE-COLD SUMMER DRINKS; THE FLOWERS PROVIDING A COLORFUL GARNISH TO CRISP AND CRUNCHY SALADS; THE YOUNG LEAVES LIGHTLY BOILED AND SERVED AS AN ALTERNATIVE TO SPINACH . . .

The bright blue, star-shaped flowers of borage make it one of the prettiest of herb plants, though the leaves, dark green, downy, and with no fragrance, are unremarkable. It is a hardy annual, a native of northern Europe, and grows well in the temperate regions of North America.

HISTORY

Borage has, over the centuries, been accredited with legendary powers. Pliny called it *euphrosinum* because it was said to bring happiness and joy wherever it grew. The ancient Greeks and Romans looked to it for comfort and courage, and this belief in its capabilities was revived in the Middle Ages. Gerard, in his *Herball*, quotes, "I, Borage, bring always courage."

Borage leaves are used to make a soothing tisane, while the flowers are traditionally used to decorate summer drinks.

IDENTIFICATION

The leaves have a flavor reminiscent of cucumber. The plant grows to a height of about 18 inches, with a spread of 12 inches. It has a messy, straggling habit, compensated for by the cloud of blue flowers that grow in arched clusters and persist throughout the summer months.

CULTIVATION

When borage is happy it will self-seed all over the garden, and the seedlings will survive provided that a really severe winter does not follow. It is considered to be a hardy annual in all areas except the very coldest, and seed is sown afresh each spring. Seed can be sown *in situ*, or even started earlier in boxes, although it is difficult in some areas to transplant unless the seedlings are planted out when very small. Leave 18 inches between the plants so that their spreading stems do not become entangled. Borage thrives in a sunny situation and well drained light soil, and will grow in pots or window boxes. A seed or two sown in fall in a pot inside will provide fresh leaves throughout the winter, but need lots of light to thrive.

HOW TO USE

Borage flowers and leaves are the traditional decoration for gin-based summer cocktails, and may be set in ice cubes to garnish other drinks. The flowers may be used to garnish salads, and candied for cake decoration.

Borage tisane, an infusion of the leaves, may be taken to ease coughs, and the leaves may be used as a poultice to alleviate muscular strains.

Left:

With their light blue, star-shaped flowers and downy leaves, borage plants make a focal point in any herb border.

Brassica juncea

MUSTARD

THE SEED GERMINATED INSIDE AND SERVED AS A PUNGENT SALAD; THE TINY ROUND SEED USED AS A PICKLING SPICE FOR COLORFUL AND HIGH-TEXTURED VEGETABLES; THE POWDER ADDING A DASH OF SPICE TO SALAD DRESSINGS AND CREAMY EGG DISHES . . .

There are three types of mustard: *Brassica nigra*, black mustard, which can reach a height of 10 feet and was the main type grown commercially until some 40 years ago; *B. juncea*, brown mustard, which, growing to only 4½ feet, is more suitable for modern methods of harvesting; and *B. alba*, white mustard, a much milder form and the one beloved of schoolchildren, who grow it as "mustard and cress".

The pungency of the herb is due to an essential oil which forms only when the dry mustard powder is mixed with water. It is not present in the dry seed – which is why the seed does not have the "bite" of made mustard – nor in the dry powder.

HISTORY

The Romans used mustard freely, soaking the dry seed in wine, and it is mentioned several times in the Bible. The name is thought to come from the Latin, *mustum ardens*, or burning must. Shakespeare includes several references to the herb, and places its commercial production accurately in Gloucester-shire, England, a main center of its growth, when he writes of "Tewkesbury mustard." It used to be ground by millers and sold as dry powder or paste in earthenware pots covered with parchment.

IDENTIFICATION

Brown mustard, sometimes called juncea mustard, has a mass of small, four-petaled yellow flowers that form a dense carpet over the fields where they grow. It originates from China, India, and Poland. White mustard, which comes from the Mediterranean region, has a less distinctive flavor.

CULTIVATION

All three types of mustard may be grown outside from seed sown in spring. It likes a moist soil and a sunny position. Harvest the seedpods in late summer, before they dry, and allow the seed to ripen in the pods. Store the seed in airtight jars, away from strong light. Seed may also be grown inside. The traditional way for children to grow it is on a piece of folded cloth placed in a saucer and kept permanently moist – a process known as chitting. It will produce tasty and pungent shoots about 4 inches tall.

HOW TO USE

Mustard powder should be mixed with cold water. Boiling water kills the enzymes and produces a bitter flavor. Dry mustard powder is added to salad dressings to give them pungency, added to egg and cheese dishes, and can be rubbed over the skin of meat before roasting. White mustard seed is a preservative used in pickling, either alone or as an ingredient in mixed pickling spice.

Ready-made mustards vary according to regional traditions. Dijon mustard is made from black mustard seed mixed with wine and spices; Bordeaux mustard contains the seed husks; English mustard is usually a mixture of black and white seeds blended with wheat flour. Whole-grain mustards, with their coarse granular texture, are becoming more popular.

A mustard bath, where the powder is mixed with hot water, is comforting for sore and aching feet and relaxing and reviving for the entire body.

Calendula officinalis

POT MARIGOLD

MARMALADE-COLORED PETALS, SCATTERED OVER A
GREEN SALAD AS A SPICY GARNISH; WHOLE FLOWERS
USED IN THE MEDIEVAL FASHION TO DECORATE
DISHES OF MEAT AND FISH; THE PETALS STREWN INTO
CREAMY CUSTARDS TO COLOR THEM GOLDEN AND
ADD A HINT OF SPICE . . .

The sunshine-gold marigold flowers are a familiar sight in
cottage and country gardens and in colorful window boxes.
The plant is a native of southern Europe but flourishes in
cool, temperate climates. It was once treasured for its many
culinary uses; the petals have a pungent, spicy flavor, and the
leaves have a rather bitter aftertaste. A hardy annual, the pot
marigold has a long flowering period, though not usually as
long as its French popular name, *tous les mois*, would suggest.

HISTORY
Fresh or dried petals have been used as a saffron substitute
since Roman times, and dried petals were sold from barrels
by spice merchants in the Middle Ages for culinary and medicinal use.

IDENTIFICATION
The plants can grow to a height of 9 inches, with a 6-inch
spread. The pointed-oval leaves, which may be about 5 inches
long, are slightly hairy. The flowers, either single or duble,
are yellow or bright orange with raised yellow centers.

CULTIVATION
A packet of pot marigold seed sown in the spring provides a
sizeable bed or border edging of these vigorous plants. They
like a rich, light soil and a sunny position, and grow well in
troughs and pots. Pot marigolds readily seed themselves.

HOW TO USE
The petals, with their slight aromatic bitterness, are used in
fish and meat soups, rice dishes, cakes, desserts, and salads
and, commercially, as a coloring for cheese and butter. In
medieval times, the whole flowers were popular as a garnish.

Medicinally, the petals were used to heal wounds and to
treat conjunctivitis, while the leaves were felt to relieve the
effects of bee stings.

An infusion of the petals may be used as a hair rinse to
lighten fair hair, and the petals made into a nourishing cream
for the skin.

When used together with alum, the petals give a yellow dye.

Above:

*Marigold petals give a
piquant, spicy flavor to
salads and, in the medieval
way, may be scattered over
desserts such as apple flan.*

MARIGOLD WINE

Yields 1 gallon

Ingredients

2 quarts marigolds (use *Calendula officinalis* only)
1 gallon boiling water
1 Campden tablet, crushed (sterilizer)
thinly pared peel and juice of 3 tangerines or other
large, soft citrus
thinly pared peel and juice of 1 lemon
5¾ cups sugar
1¼ cups white raisins, finely chopped
wine yeast
yeast nutrient

Preparation

Wash the flowers and put into a large container. Pour over the water, stir in the Campden tablet, and leave for 24 hours.

Draw off 1 cup of the liquid, heat to just on boiling point with the citrus peel, then pour over the sugar, stirring until dissolved. Leave to cool to blood temperature, then pour back into the bulk of the liquid together with the white raisins, citrus juice, yeast, and nutrient. Cover and leave in a warm place for 5 days to ferment, stirring twice a day.

Strain the liquid through a double thickness of muslin. Pour into a fermenting jar, fitted with a fermentation lock, and leave to continue fermenting. Rack the wine as it begins to clear.

When the wine is completely clear, bottle and store in a cool, dark, dry place for at least 6 months to mature.

CREAMY MARIGOLD CLEANSER

Ingredients

4 tablespoons olive or almond oil
2 tablespoons dried pot marigold flowers
few drops of violet, orange blossom or rose water

Preparation

Warm the oil in a bowl placed over a saucepan of hot water. Stir in the dried flowers and continue to heat gently for 30 minutes.

Remove the bowl from the heat and allow the oil to cool. Stir in the flower water.

Far left:

Pot marigolds, Calendula officinalis *– their daisy-shaped bright orange flowers are the stars of any mixed border.*

Carum carvi

CARAWAY

ADMINISTERED TO BOTH LOVERS AND POULTRY IN
MEDIEVAL TIMES TO PREVENT THEIR STRAYING; THE
SEEDS ADDING THEIR PUNGENT FLAVOR TO
VEGETABLES . . .

Above:

*A slender and straggly
plant, caraway has delicate
clusters of white flowers
and small, feathery leaves.*

Caraway is a two-in-one plant. The bright green, feathery
leaves have a mild flavor, somewhere between that of parsley
and dill, while the seeds, a spice, have a strong aroma and
pungent taste. The plant is grown commercially for its seed in
northern Europe, the United States, and North Africa. A flavoring for use in baked goods and sweets is made from the essential oil distilled from the dry, ripe seed.

HISTORY

Right:

*Caraway, one of a large
family of umbellifers, is at
its most effective when
grown in a large clump.*

The plant was extensively used by the Romans and was well
established in English kitchens in the Middle Ages, when it
was cooked with fruit, especially spit-roast apples, and in cakes
and bread. The leaves were chopped into soups and salads. In
Germany and Austria – still the prime users of the plant – the
seeds were cooked with vegetables, especially cabbage and its
preserved form, sauerkraut.

IDENTIFICATION

A biennial, the plant grows to a height of up to 2 feet, with a
spread of 12 inches, and has thick, tapering roots rather like
those of parsnip. The leaves resemble those of the carrot in
shape. The flowers, in umbellifer clusters, are white tinged
with pink and appear in mid-summer. The pointed-oval seeds
are dark brown, almost black.

CULTIVATION

Seedlings do not transplant well, so sow *in situ* in spring or
fall. Caraway thrives in all but the most humid warm regions,
and does best from fall-sown seed because the germination is
quicker from fresh seed. Subsequently the little plants need to
be thinned so that they are about 6 inches apart, and may be
grown in either groups or rows. But, when they are grown for
their carrot-like roots it is best to do so in rows and treat them
as a vegetable. They will grow in almost any well drained soil
but need plenty of sun to produce seed of an acceptable
flavor.

HOW TO USE

The leaves may be used in salads and soups, the seeds in
baked goods, in dumplings, cream cheese, and meat dishes
such as goulash and pork casserole. The roots can be boiled
as a vegetable and served with a white sauce.

The leaves, seeds, and roots can be used as an aid to
digestion.

C h r y s a n t h e m u m   p a r t h e n i u m

FEVERFEW

A FEW OF THE YOUNGEST, TENDEREST LEAVES MADE
INTO SANDWICHES TO WARD OFF MIGRAINE; A TISANE
OF FRESH OR DRIED LEAVES TAKEN AS A TONIC; AN
INFUSION OF THE FLOWERS PATTED LIGHTLY ON THE
SKIN AS A SOFTENER . . .

With its bright lime green or yellowy-green leaves that retain
their color through the winter, feverfew is a year-round
decorative garden plant. It is low growing, bushy, and vigorous,
quickly thickening up, spreading, and self-seeding. The white
flowers, which may be like single or double daisies, are particularly pretty and dry well for flower arranging.

HISTORY
Its medicinal uses are well chronicled by Gerard who, in his
Herball, said that the dried plant was useful for those "that are
giddie in the head ... melancholike and pensive;" and by
Culpeper, who recommended it for "all pains of the head
coming of a cold cause."

IDENTIFICATION
Various forms of the plant may grow to a height of anywhere
from 9 inches to 2 feet. The deeply cut leaves are brightly
colored, and have a sharp, unpleasantly bitter taste. The
flowers, which are produced through the summer and into
mid-fall, are thick and daisy-like, with yellow centers.

CULTIVATION
The plant will thrive in the poorest of soils, even in paving
cracks and walls. Ideally, it likes a well-drained soil and a
sunny position. You can easily grow it from seed or by root
division.

HOW TO USE
The plant's bitter taste rules out culinary uses, but is worth
tolerating for its medicinal properties. The fresh or dried
leaves can be particularly effective (made into sandwiches) as
a cure for migraine, and as a tonic.

The flowers are used in some skin preparations.

Above:
*Feverfew, whose pungent,
bitter leaves are used in the
treatment of migraine, has
small, daisy-like flowers.*

Left:
*With its bright, sharp green
leaves, feverfew is an
attractive border plant.
Another form has even
brighter leaves which are
almost yellow.*

Coriandrum sativum

CORIANDER

THE TINY ROUND SEEDS CRUSHED TO A PASTE WITH
CHOPPED PARSLEY AND OLIVE OIL AND RUBBED INTO
LAMB BEFORE ROASTING; THE SEEDS USED TO GIVE
THE CHARACTERISTIC "BITE" TO MUSHROOMS *A LA
GRECQUE;* THE LEAVES ADDED JUST BEFORE SERVING
SPICY CURRIES . . .

Both the green feathery leaves (sometimes known as cilantro)
and the spherical seeds of coriander are indispensable in the
kitchen, especially to anyone who is fond of curries. Bunches
of coriander, which looks like flat-leaved parsley, are sold in
many markets, especially where there is an Asian or Greek
community. The seed is sold both whole or ground, and is a
major ingredient in curry powder. It has a sweet taste reminiscent of orange peel.

HISTORY

Coriander seed was mentioned in the Bible, where it was
likened to manna, but its use goes back much farther in time.
The herb was used both in cooking and medicine in the ancient
European cultures, and in South America, India, and China
many thousands of years ago. The Romans took it to Britain,
where it was much used in Elizabethan times.

IDENTIFICATION

The plant grows to a height of 2 feet, with a spread of 9 inches.
The bright green leaves are fan shaped and become more
feathery towards the top of the plant. The flowers, which bloom
from mid- to late summer, are small and white, formed in
umbel-like clusters. The pale brown roots are fibrous and
tapering, shaped rather like a carrot.

CULTIVATION

Coriander grows best in a dry atmosphere – in fact it is difficult to grow in damp or humid areas, and needs a good dry
summer at the very least if a reasonable crop is to be obtained.
Choose a sunny place and sow seed *in situ* once all danger of
frost has passed. Alternatively, sow into decorative containers
and continue to cultivate as a container plant on an apartment
balcony, sunny patio or yard. The stems are weak and the
plants tend to lo'l about and appear top heavy, so either add a
twiggy stake or give it a companion to lean against!

HOW TO USE

The leaves do not dry well, but may be frozen. They are used
in curries; ground to a paste with olive oil and the ground
seed as a covering for roast lamb in marinades; sparingly – as
they are rather bitter – in salads; and mixed with coconut and
green chilies in a classic Indian chutney. The seeds, which
may be roasted to bring out the full flavor, are widely used in
curries and casseroles, in sausages, with fish and all *à la
Grecque* dishes. They are also included in mixed pickling spice.

Medicinally, the herb may be taken as a digestive and for
the treatment of colic.

Left:

*Coriander leaves are used
in the preparation of
curries and many dishes of
Middle-Eastern origin.*

MARINATED SMOKED FISH
FILLETS

Serves 6 as an appetizer, 3 as a main dish

Ingredients

12 ounches smoked fish fillets
1 medium onion, thinly sliced
2 teaspoons coriander seeds, crushed
2 bay leaves
freshly ground black pepper
¾ cup sunflower oil
4 tablespoons red wine vinegar
1 tablespoon soft brown sugar
grated peel of 1 lemon
2 teaspoons mustard powder
1 lemon, sliced
sprigs of fresh coriander

The long marinating period revolutionizes the flavor of the fish. Have a good supply of crusty bread to mop up the delicious juices.

Preparation

Using a sharp knife, remove the skins from the smoked fish. Slice the fillets diagonally into long strips. Layer in a shallow, wide dish, together with the onion, crushed coriander seeds, bay leaves, and black pepper.

—

In a screw-top jar, shake together the oil, vinegar, brown sugar, lemon peel, and mustard powder until well blended and dissolved.

—

Pour the dressing over the fillets. Cover tightly with plastic wrap and refrigerate for 2–5 days (the longer the better). Turn the fillets occasionally in the marinade.

—

Serve garnished with lemon slices and sprigs of fresh coriander.

Above:

A patch of delicately colored dianthus or pinks is a perfect edging for a herbaceous border or herb garden.

Right:

The clove pink was known in Victorian times as the gillyflower, or July flower.

Dianthus caryophyllus

PINK

THE FLOWERS STREWN IN SYRUP TO SERVE WITH FRUIT SALADS AND COMPOTES, OR SET IN ICE CUBES TO SERVE WITH TINGLING-COLD SUMMER DRINKS; THE DRIED FLOWERS — PINK, RED, CRIMSON, OR WHITE — ADD COLOR AND FRAGRANCE...

The garden pink or border carnation, romantically known as the gillyflower or July flower in Elizabethan and Victorian times, is a familiar and pretty cottage-garden plant. It grows wild in southern Europe and India, and has become naturalized in Britain. The flowers may be single or double and come in all shades of pink and red, from shell pink to carmine.

HISTORY
The flowers have been used for cooking and perfumes for more than 2,000 years. In the Middle Ages, pinks were used in England as a clove substitute to spice wine and ale, when they were known as "sops."

IDENTIFICATION
The plant grows to 12–24 inches, and may have a spread of 10 inches. The stems are erect, straight, and tough; the leaves long, slender, and greyish to silvery green. The flowers, about 1 inch across, are formed singly or in clusters and have a strong, clove-like aroma. Some have cut or intricately frilled petals and splashes or flashes of dual color. Many hybridized version are available.

CULTIVATION
The plant, a perennial, thrives in a poor but well-drained soil, and will even grow on walls or between paving slabs. It may be grown from seed planted in late spring, but is more usually propagated by root division or layering in late summer.

HOW TO USE
The flowers have a sweet, spicy taste and are used to flavor syrups, especially for fruit salad, sauces, creams, jellies, butter, wine, fruit drinks, and salad dressings. They are candied to decorate cakes and desserts, and used to garnish salads.

They may be used to scent toilet waters, and in potpourri and herbal sleep pillows. The flowerheads may be arranged with other herbs in informal country-style groups, and the seedheads used in long-lasting decorations such as herb rings and swags. The seeds may be tied in pouches and included in wedding wreath designs, or glued to a pre-formed foam ball to make a spice tree.

Foeniculum vulgare

FENNEL

THE SOFT THREAD-LIKE LEAVES WRAPPED AROUND
HERRING OR MACKEREL FOR BAKING, CHOPPED INTO A
STUFFING TO COOK WITH TROUT, OR USED
GENEROUSLY IN MARINADE FOR PORK; THE SEEDS
BAKED WITH CHOPPED BLACK OLIVES IN BREAD TO
SERVE PLOUGHMAN STYLE, WITH CHEESE AND COLD
BEER . . .

With its umbels of minute yellow flowers and dark green or
bronze wispy leaves, fennel is a decorative addition to a
herbaceous border, where, because of its size, it makes a
good background plant. For centuries the herb has been associated in cooking with fish and used medicinally as a digestive.
The seeds are chewed as a breath freshener, particularly
appropriate after eating curries. Sweet or Roman fennel, the
herb, should not be confused with Florence fennel (*finocchio*),
the vegetable grown for its creamy-white bulbous root.

HISTORY

Fennel is native to southern Europe, and was extensively used
by the Romans. Its use in England was widespread before the
Norman conquest. Its partnership with fish was so well established, on fast days poor people are said to have eaten the
fennel without fish.

IDENTIFICATION

The plant dominates any border, growing to a height of 5 feet,
with a spread of 2½ feet. The stems are pale green, multi-
branched, and ridged. The leaves, soft and frondy, are formed
like giant hands and have an anise-like flavor. The seeds –
which are flat, ridged, and oval – form in late summer and
have a more pronounced taste.

Above:
*The leaves and dried stems
of fennel and bronze fennel
are extremely good with
poached and grilled fish.*

CULTIVATION

Fennel is a tall plant suitable for the back of the herb border. Seed should be sown in the late spring. To maintain a continuous supply of fresh leaves throughout the season, sow a few seeds in succession with about a 10-day interval between sowings. It can be grown as an annual, although the established roots make good plants that overwinter easily. Divide such established roots in the fall after the seed has been harvested.

HOW TO USE

The leaves are used with pork, veal and fish, in fish stock, sauces and stuffings, and in mayonnaise and salad dressings. The dried stalks are placed under grilled or barbecued fish to impart flavor. The seeds are used as a spice, particularly in bread, cookies, and biscuits. At the two-leaf (cotyledon) stage, the seedlings make a pungent salad, reminiscent of mustard.

Medicinally, the leaves and dried seeds are used for flatulence and in gripe waters, which are still popular for babies' colic, while an infusion of the leaves may be used for eyestrain.

Above:

Its tall, curving stems and its dense cluster of soft feathery leaves make fennel and bronze fennel ideal back-of-the-border plants.

BAKED FISH WITH LIME & HERB BUTTER

Serves 4

Ingredients

¼ cup butter

4 medium or 1 large fish, cleaned

1 teaspoon fennel seeds

2 limes

1 cup medium-sweet red wine

salt and freshly ground black pepper

sprigs of fresh fennel

Oven temperature: 400°

The subtle flavors of fennel and lime blend beautifully with red mullet, snapper, or rainbow trout. For a delicious variation, substitute orange and vermouth for the lime and wine.

Preparation

Preheat the oven. Lightly butter a shallow oven-proof dish. Place the fish in the bottom. Dot with the remaining butter and then sprinkle with the fennel seeds.

—

Using a vegetable peeler, cut several strips of the lime peel and put among the fish. Squeeze over the juice of the limes and pour the wine over the fish.

—

Season well with salt and freshly ground black pepper. Cover tightly with foil and bake for about 25 minutes, or until the fish is cooked through and flakes easily when tested with the tip of a knife.

—

Serve the fish with some of its juices, garnished with a few sprigs of fresh fennel and topped with a slice of chilled butter mixed with herbs, if wished.

Hyssopus officinalis 🗄️ 🥣 🧴

HYSSOP

FRESH LEAVES USED SPARINGLY AS A SCATTER-
GARNISH FOR TOMATO OR CUCUMBER SALADS; DRIED
LEAVES ADDED TO SOUPS; THE BRIGHT BLUE FLOWERS
USED, AS THEY WERE GENERATIONS AGO, TO GARNISH
COLD MEAT DISHES . . .

Far left:
A dense, healthy hyssop
plant, its leaves a tender
green, is a fine sight in any
herb garden.

This decorative and long-lasting herb is an attractive one to grow. Native to southern Europe, the Near East, and southern Russia, it is a garden escape in the United States. It has a slightly bitter flavor with over-tones of mint, and was so widely known in ancient times Dioscorides wrote that it needed no description.

HISTORY

Hyssop was used in all the Mediterranean countries in pre-Christian times, and is mentioned in the Bible. In his *Herball*, Gerard records that he grew all kinds in his garden; while Culpeper recommended it, boiled with figs, as an excellent gargle. In self-help medicine, a tisane of fresh or dried hyssop leaves was taken as a cure for rheumatism.

IDENTIFICATION

The plant grows to 2 feet tall, with a spread of around half that. The leaves are about 1 inch long, pointed oval, and dark green. The flowers, which bloom from mid-summer to mid-fall, are purple blue, ¼ inch long, and carried in long, narrow spikes. The stems, flowers, and leaves all give off a strong aroma.

CULTIVATION

Hyssop is propagated by seed sown in spring, or by cuttings taken in the same season or very early in the summer, and rooted in damp peaty soil in a shaded place. For edging, plant out the rooted cuttings in late summer about 12 inches apart, and do not clip for the following summer, but leave the job for 18 months.

Hyssop revels in light, fairly dry, warm soil and does especially well in windowboxes. It is far hardier than is generally realized. Cut growth down in the fall to prevent rough winds ripping the plant from its foothold.

HOW TO USE

The fresh or dried leaves and flowers may be added to soups, ragouts, casseroles, and sausages. Fresh leaves may be used sparingly in salads. The herb is an ingredient of Chartreuse liqueur.

Medicinally, hyssop is used for coughs, colds, bronchitis, and as a gargle for sore throats.

Fresh and dried leaves were used as a strewing herb, and may be used in potpourri, in insect-repellant sachets, and in rinsing water for laundry.

Above:
Pluck off a few of the long,
slender hyssop leaves for
use in salads, sausages, and
casseroles.

Iris germanica

ORRIS ROOT

THE DRIED POWDER, WITH ITS FRAGRANCE OF SWEET VIOLETS, USED AS A FIXATIVE IN THE MAKING OF POTPOURRI, SLEEP PILLOW BLENDS AND LAVENDER-BAG MIXTURES . . .

Spectacular as the flowers are, it is the root or rhizome of the Florentine iris that is the valuable part of the plant. The name (orris) derives from the Greek word for rainbow, indicating the range of flower colors.

HISTORY

Orris root originates from southern Europe, and became naturalized in Iran and northern India. It has been identified in a wall painting of an Egyptian temple dating from 1500 BC. It was at one time used as a purgative, but is not now used medicinally.

IDENTIFICATION

The long and slender plant grows to a height of 3 feet, while its straight, fleshy, and erect stems are wrapped in long, pointed, sword-shaped leaves. The flowers are about 4 inches across, and may be white, tinged with purple or with a yellow beard. The bulbous and fleshy rhizome is white under the skin and smells strongly of violets. The plant has small fibrous roots.

Below:

The long, sword-shaped leaves of Iris germanica *form a neat, tight fan shape.*

Above:

The dried root of the iris plant, known as orris root, is used as a fixative in pot-pourri blends.

CULTIVATION

The rhizomes are divided in late spring and should be taken with a bud or shoot in place. They prefer deep, fertile, well-drained soil and a position in full sun. They should be planted half above and half below the soil, and divided every four or five years. For dried orris root, lift the rhizomes in autumn and hang them in a warm place. The fragrance develops as the rhizomes wither and dry.

HOW TO USE

The ground powder made from the dried root is used as a fixative in potpourri, in talcum powder, bath preparations, and dry shampoos.

Laurus nobilis

BAY

A SPRAY OF BAY LEAVES GARNISHING THE TOP OF A
GLAZED TERRINE; A FRESH OR DRIED LEAF FLAVORING
A HEARTY STEW OR A DELICATE CUSTARD; THE DRIED
LEAVES BOUND ON TO A TWIG RING TO MAKE AN
EVERGREEN KITCHEN DECORATION . . .

Bay leaves are among the most versatile of herbs, and the
plants, if regularly clipped, rank among the most decorative of
shrubs. The glossy and sweetly scented leaves are indispensable in both French and Mediterranean cooking, a traditional
ingredient in bouquet garni, and a "must" in marinades, *court
bouillon*, stocks, and pickles.

HISTORY

The bay tree came originally from Asia Minor, and was established around the ancient cultures of the Mediterranean.
Dedicated to the god Apollo, it was the laurel referred to in
the crown of laurel leaves presented as a symbol of wisdom
and victory in ancient Greece and Rome, the origin of the
circlet of leaves worn by victorious motor racing drivers today.
The French word *baccalaureat*, for examinations, and the
term "bachelor," for academic degrees, both derive from the
Latin for laurel berry, *bacca laureus*.

IDENTIFICATION

Bay leaves are flat, pointed oval, about 3 inches long, dark
green, and glossy. They retain a somewhat balsamic scent, and
the wood, too, is strongly aromatic. In ideal conditions, the
shrubby trees may grow to 25 feet tall and up to 6 feet across.
The stems are tough and woody, and have a grey bark. The
flowers, which appear in late spring, are small, yellow, and
rather insiginificant.

CULTIVATION

Cuttings taken with a heel in early summer (when the new
spring growth has hardened a little) and made about 4–6
inches long are the most reliable method of propagation.
Insert them in pans or pots, potting up separately once the
roots are established, and keep them thus for a year or so
before planting out. (Layering of established plants in summer
is an alternative method of propagation.) Once plants are
growing well, an occasional spray with water helps to keep
the leaves clean and shining.

HOW TO USE

Bay leaves are used in all branches of cooking – in soups,
stews, casseroles, stocks, syrups, sauces, and as a garnish.
   An infusion of the leaves may be taken for flatulence.
   The dried leaves are crumbled into potpourri. To dry the
leaves, simply hang them in bunches in a warm, dry place.

Above:
The pointed-oval, glossy
leaves of the bay tree are a
fragrant addition to sweet
and savoury dishes of all
kinds.

Right:

Left to its own devices, a bay tree will spread far and wide. The trees are perfect candidates for clipping into neat topiary shapes.

PATATAS BRAVAS

Serves 4

Ingredients

1 onion, chopped
2 tablespoons olive oil
1 bay leaf
2 red chilies
2 teaspoons crushed garlic
1 tablespoon tomato paste
1 tablespoon sugar
1 tablespoon soy sauce
1 pound can plum tomatoes, chopped
1 glass of white wine
salt and black pepper
8 medium potatoes

Oven temperature: 450°

The sauce for this dish should be slightly sweet and the flavor of the tomatoes should not dominate it.

Preparation

To make the sauce, sweat the onions in the oil with the bay leaf.

—

When soft, add the chilies, garlic, tomato paste, sugar, and soy sauce. Sweat for a further 5 minutes on a low heat.

—

Add the chopped tomatoes and white wine. Stir, bring to the boil and simmer for 10 minutes. Season to taste.

—

To prepare the potatoes, cut as you would for roast potatoes. Place the potatoes on a greased baking sheet, season well and brush with melted butter. Roast in the hot oven until golden.

—

Reheat the tomato sauce, pour over the potatoes and serve immediately.

Right:
*Lavender flowers have
many culinary, cosmetic,
and domestic uses, and are
an invaluable ingredient
in potpourri.*

Lavandula angustifolia

LAVENDER

BUNCHES OF LAVENDER HANGING TO DRY IN A
CORNER; A BASKET OF HEADILY SCENTED LAVENDER
FLOWERS DECORATING A BEDROOM OR BATHROOM; A
"BOUQUET" OF FLOWERS STREWN IN SYRUP TO POUR
OVER SWEET CAKES AND PASTRIES . . .

Lavender is a traditional cottage-garden plant, its grey-green
spiky foliage and spires of purple-blue flowers providing color
throughout the year. It is native to the Mediterranean and
grows in profusion in the sun-baked *maquis* region of
southern France.

HISTORY

The Greeks and Romans used this highly aromatic plant to
make perfumes and ointments. Since the Middle Ages, the
dried flowers have been one of the main ingredients of potpourri; fresh sprigs were included in herbal bunches, known
as tussie mussies, to mask unpleasant household odors and
ward off fevers. Bunches of lavender were sold on city streets
in Victorian times. "Won't you buy my pretty lavender?" was
one of the traditional street cries of London.

IDENTIFICATION

The plant may grow to a height of 3 feet, but there are dwarf
forms for edging which reach only about 10 inches. The stems
are thick and woody, and become straggly if left unpruned.
The leaves are long (about 3 inches), spiky, and very narrow.
The tiny tubular flowers are carried on long spikes in thick
round-the-stem clusters. The fibrous roots are shallow and
wide spreading.

CULTIVATION

Propagate from cuttings of strong new growth in summer or autumn, and once rooted plant them out in a well drained, rather poor soil. The bushes tend to look after themselves and respond to an annual haircut in fall after flowering, or in early spring. Bushes tend to straggle as they mature and it is often necessary to cut back severely in fall to generate a strong growth the following spring. It is wise to maintain a supply of young plants.

HOW TO USE

Fresh lavender flowers may be used to flavor syrup for jellies and fruit salad, and milk and cream for desserts. They may also be candied to decorate cakes and puddings.

Bunches of lavender are said to ward off insects, and an infusion of the flowers may help relieve insect bites.

Fresh or dried flowers are used in rinsing water for clothes and hair.

Because of their sweet, pungent smell, the dried flowers and seeds are a frequent ingredient of potpourris, herbal sleep pillows, and sachets. Dried lavender stems are used to weave decorative baskets and bowls.

Right:

Whether grown commercially in a field, as a dense hedge or as a border plant, lavender is one of the most attractive and fragrant of herbs.

SIMPLE LAVENDER SOAP

Ingredients
10 tablespoons finely grated castille soap
8 tablespoons boiling water
2 tablespoons crushed dried lavender flowers
4 drops of lavender oil

Preparation
Melt the soap in the water in a bowl placed over a saucepan of hot water, stirring frequently, until smooth.

—

Crush the flowers to a powder and take the bowl off the saucepan of hot water. Stir the flowers into the soap with the oil.

—

Pour into a bottle and label.

Levisticum officinale

LOVAGE

A CLEAR, SPARKLING MEAT BROTH FLAVORED WITH
YOUNG LEMON-SCENTED SHOOTS OF LOVAGE; A
SAUCE MADE WITH THE CHOPPED LEAVES AND SERVED
WITH POACHED WHITE FISH; THE CELERY-FLAVORED
SEEDS BAKED IN COOKIES TO SERVE WITH
CHEESE . . .

Lovage was much used as a herb in Britain during the Middle
Ages, and then, like so many others, went out of fashion for
several centuries. It is the tallest of the umbellifers, reaching
over 6 feet, and makes an attractive back-of-the-border addition. All parts of the plant – leaves, stems, and seeds – can be
used in the kitchen, and so it well repays its keep.

HISTORY

A native of southern Europe, lovage was known to the Greeks
and Romans, and was recommended by Culpeper in his mid-
seventeenth century herbal. He advised that the bruised leaves,
fried in hog's lard and applied hot to the area, will quickly
break "any blotch or boil." The herb was once thought to be
an aphrodisiac, and was used by witches in their love potions.

IDENTIFICATION

With its bright green, hand-shaped leaflets and thickly ridged
hollow stems, the plant looks rather like over-grown celery,
and gives off a distinct celery-like aroma. The flowers, which
bloom in mid- to late summer, are small, yellow, and formed
in umbrella-like clusters. The seeds are flat, oval, and deeply
ridged. The plant reaches a height of 5 feet.

CULTIVATION

Lovage is one of the few herbs tolerant to shade; it seems to
adapt to both full sun or partial shade with impunity. It will
reward good cultural care by lasting for several years, when
the root stock becomes stout and woody and can be used as a
casserole vegetable after the bitter-tasting skin has been
removed.

It will grow in most places where it gets the period of
dormancy which is necessary to complete the growth cycle.
Sow seed in late summer once it has ripened, either in a pot
or *in situ*, and retain only a few of the best seedlings. One or
two lovage plants are sufficient for the needs of most families,
but more can be grown for garden decoration. Keep the
seedlings watered in both fall and spring, and take care that
the young lovage plants are not allowed to dry out.

HOW TO USE

The leaves may be used to flavor soups, casseroles, sauces,
and marinades, or lightly cooked as a green vegetable. The
stems are candied as angelica, and the seeds are often used to
flavor bread, cookies, and biscuits.

An infusion can be used as a diuretic, to relieve flatulence,
and as an antiseptic.

The bright leaves are attractive components of herbal
arrangements, and they may be used as a backing for flat
posies and sprays.

Above:
*The large, fleshy leaves of
lovage may be lightly
cooked as a vegetable, and
the stems candied and used
in the same way as
angelica.*

Left:
*Lovage, which grows to a
height of 6 feet, is a tall,
stately plant topped by
clusters of greenish-yellow
flowers.*

IDENTIFICATION

The plant is a vigorous grower that will readily spread through the border. It reaches a height of 3 feet, with a spread of 2 feet. The oval, almost heart-shaped, leaves have slightly serrated edges and a pronounced network of veins; they can be up to 2½ inches long and 1½ inches across. The flowers, which bloom from mid- to late summer are small, white, and insignificant.

CULTIVATION

Although slow to germinate, seed is otherwise easy to grow, and as it is so fine it hardly needs covering. A quicker method of propagation is to take cuttings in late spring and plant them out once they are established in warm districts, or in the following spring. A moist soil in a sunny spot enhances the essential oil of this plant, ridding it of the slightly musty overtones that develop during dry seasons or on light, dry soils. It is especially good, in both appearance and aroma, in the controlled conditions of containers. Cut back to soil level in the fall to encourage young fresh growth and good fragrance.

Lemon balm is happiest in moderately warm regions, where it grows a little more lushly but it does not like great humidity and needs a cold winter to give of its best.

HOW TO USE

The fresh leaves may be used in salads, candied for cake decoration, and used to garnish fish and other dishes. Add them at the last minute to summer drinks and fruit salads – after long infusion they turn unpleasantly brown – and, in recipes, as a lemon peel substitute.

An infusion of the leaves makes a refreshing skin toner and can be used in water to rinse clothes.

The dry leaves lend a refreshing lemony scent to potpourri blends.

Melissa officinalis

LEMON BALM

THE BRIGHT YELLOW-GREEN LEAVES STREWN IN SYRUP FOR FRUIT SALADS AND COMPOTES; FLOATING IN WHITE WINE OR STRAWBERRY CUPS; SCATTERED OVER GREEN SALAD, OR SHAKEN, JUST BEFORE SERVING, IN SALAD DRESSINGS TO IMPART A LEMONY FLAVOR . . .

Balm is an attractive herb with yellow or variegated leaves smelling strongly of lemons. It is a great addition to any garden since it maintains a strong attraction for bees. Indeed, it used to be said that a swarm of bees would never desert a hive if a lemon balm plant was close by. A tisane made from the leaves, known as melissa tea, is said to relieve tiredness, sooth headaches, and have a calming effect on the nerves. In this capacity, it was a popular drink with Victorian ladies.

HISTORY

Lemon balm is native to southern Europe and has been cultivated for over 2,000 years. The Romans brought it to Britain, where it was widely grown in the Middle Ages, during which time melissa honey was popular as a sugar substitute.

Mentha pulegium

PENNYROYAL

HERBY SAUSAGES AROMATIC WITH ITS STRONG AND
MINT-LIKE FLAVOR; A FEW DRIED LEAVES ADDED TO
"LINEN BAGS" TO HANG IN WARDROBES . . .

Pennyroyal, a herbaceous perennial and a close relation of
mint, has a strong, bitter, minty taste some people find
unpleasant. It has a completely different growing habit than
mint, its prostrate stems creeping along the ground and forming an effective, dense ground cover that can be used as a
lawn. It is a native of Europe where it grows freely in damp,
shady places and is also found in North and South America.

HISTORY

In spite of its bitter aroma and flavor, pennyroyal was widely
used as a culinary herb by the Greeks and Romans. It had its
domestic uses, too, and, as its name implies (*pulegium* is
derived from *pulex*, the Latin for flea), was used as an insect
repellant.

IDENTIFICATION

Each prostrate plant is capable of spreading at least 12 inches
along the ground. The leaves, around ¼–½ inches long, are
dark green, oval, and may be toothed. The flowers, which
appear from mid- to late summer, are purple and borne in
tight clusters at leaf joints around the stem.

CULTIVATION

A good ground cover herb, pennyroyal enjoys a damp position
where there is a good deal of shade. Plant it among paving
slabs where its roots can run about in the cool soil. Both the
creeping and the upright sort will enhance a garden patio
corner or a herb garden pathway. It should be lifted and moved
inside in areas where the temperature falls below –5°.

HOW TO USE

The leaves may be used sparingly in place of mint, but have
more application medicinally and domestically.

The can be used to relieve insect bites and stings, to ward
off insects – as a moth repellant in drawers, for instance – and
in the treatment of headaches, colds, and sickness.

The leaves have been used as a strewing herb.

Note that pennyroyal should not be taken during the
months of pregnancy.

Above:

*In days gone by, the tiny,
rounded leaves of
pennyroyal were used as a
strewing herb and as an
aromatic rinse for laundry.*

Above:

A selection of mints:

1 apple mint;

2 variegated apple mint;

3 black peppermint;

4 white peppermint;

5 ginger mint;

6 lemon mint;

7 basil mint;

8 eau-de-cologne mint;

9 curly garden mint.

Mentha spicata

GARDEN MINT

A LEAF OR TWO OF NEW SEASON'S MINT ADDED TO
POTATOES AND PEAS IN CELEBRATION OF THE FIRST
YOUNG CROPS; BELL PEPPERS BAKED GREEK-STYLE
WITH A RICE AND MINT STUFFING; CANDIED YOUNG
SPRIGS TO DECORATE CAKES AND DESSERTS . . .

There are many species and types of this most popular of
culinary herbs.

Spearmint, or garden mint, is the most commonly grown
"domestic" mint, which, according to variety, may have dark
green or grey-green leaves with smooth, decorative, or frilled
edges; eau-de-cologne mint (*M. citrata*) has the scent of orange
flowers and numbers orange, lavender, and bergamot mints
among its varieties; water mint (*M. aquatica*) and horse mint
(*M. longifolia*) grow in the wild and have an overpoweringly
strong aroma; while round-leaved mint (*M. rotundifolia*) has
a distinctive appearance and numbers apple mint, Bowles,
and pineapple mints in its list of varieties.

Most species are native to the Mediterranean region and
western Asia, and now grow wild throughout northern Europe
and in parts of North America. They will grow wild in the
garden, too, if their roots are not contained (in a bottomless
container sunk into the ground, such as an old bucket) and
their colonization process curtailed by vigilant thinning and
cutting back.

HISTORY

Mint was used extensively by the Greeks and Romans. Pliny
said of it that "the smell . . . does stir up the mind and the taste
to a greedy desire of meat". And it was the Romans who introduced both spearmint and mint sauce to Britain.

IDENTIFICATION

The plants, herbaceous perennials, may grow to a height of
over 18 inches, with a spread of 12 inches. They have tough,
vigorous roots and stems, which creep beneath the ground
and establish new plants along the way making this herb most
difficult to eradicate. The small, bluish-purple flowers, which
tend to bloom late in the summer, are borne in clusters on
cylindrical spires.

CULTIVATION

Mint is propagated by planting pieces of the rooted stem – known in Britain as Irishman's cuttings – about 2 inches deep in moist loamy soil, at almost any time during the growing season. Apple mint, sometimes called dryland mint in America, will tolerate less moist soil; they all like the sunlight. The plants need to be confined to their allotted space and this is best achieved by encircling the area with bricks or tiles, or pushing plastic strips into the ground to prevent their advance.

Container growing is possible provided regular watering can be assured – otherwise the containers need to be sunk into the ground. All mints can be grown inside (although they tend to become scraggy) except for apple mint which sometimes makes quite a handsome plant.

A productive mint bed in the herb or kitchen garden should be remade and moved every three or four years to reduce the likelihood of mint rust disease.

Crowns of mint plants can be boxed or potted up in winter and taken to a warm greenhouse or conservatory to force succulent fresh shoots which become available within three or four weeks.

HOW TO USE

Mint sauce, in which the chopped herb is mixed with vinegar as an accompaniment to roast lamb, is the traditional herald of a British spring. A sprig of mint can be added when cooking potatoes, peas, squash, and many other vegetables. Mint is chopped into softened butter for serving with lamb; and into apple jelly as a preserve to serve with a variety of poultry, meats, and grilled fish. Sprigs of mint are also used as a garnish, and to flavor fruit salads and summer drinks, particularly mint julep.

Mint tea, served hot or cold with a slice of lemon, is a refreshing and reviving tisane.

GRAPEFRUIT MINT SORBET

Serves 6

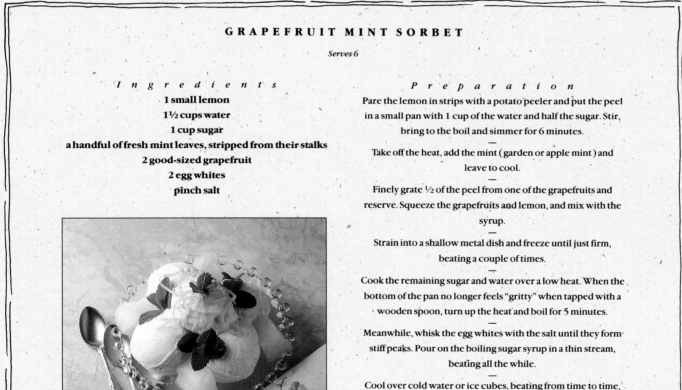

Ingredients

1 small lemon
1½ cups water
1 cup sugar
a handful of fresh mint leaves, stripped from their stalks
2 good-sized grapefruit
2 egg whites
pinch salt

Preparation

Pare the lemon in strips with a potato peeler and put the peel in a small pan with 1 cup of the water and half the sugar. Stir, bring to the boil and simmer for 6 minutes.

—

Take off the heat, add the mint (garden or apple mint) and leave to cool.

—

Finely grate ½ of the peel from one of the grapefruits and reserve. Squeeze the grapefruits and lemon, and mix with the syrup.

—

Strain into a shallow metal dish and freeze until just firm, beating a couple of times.

—

Cook the remaining sugar and water over a low heat. When the bottom of the pan no longer feels "gritty" when tapped with a wooden spoon, turn up the heat and boil for 5 minutes.

—

Meanwhile, whisk the egg whites with the salt until they form stiff peaks. Pour on the boiling sugar syrup in a thin stream, beating all the while.

—

Cool over cold water or ice cubes, beating from time to time, then beat in the grapefruit ice, broken up, and the finely grated peel. Freeze.

—

Serve garnished with fresh mint sprigs.

Monarda didyma

BERGAMOT

BERGAMOT TEA, A TISANE WITH A HISTORY, TAKEN AS A
SOOTHING AND RELAXING DRINK; THE LEAVES USED
TO GARNISH FRUIT DRINKS AND WINE CUPS; AND
DRIED TO ADD A HINT OF SPICE TO VARIOUS
POTPOURRI BLENDS . . .

The bergamots are very much an American herb, native to
North America and widely used by the American Indians. The
plant has a pleasant smell of oranges and, with its red, pinky-
red, or purple flowers, is an attractive addition to any border.
It is strongly attractive to bees. Besides the most common red
bergamot, there is wild bergamot (*M. fistulosa*), native to
southern Canada and the northern United States, and lemon
bergamot (*M. citriodora*), which, too, has a strong citrus aroma.

HISTORY

Bergamot was used by the Oswego Indians, and Oswego tea
(a name given to a type of bergamot) was made by colonists at
the time of the Boston Tea Party in order to boycott British
imports.

IDENTIFICATION

The plant, a herbaceous perennial, will grow to a height of 3
feet, with a spread of over 12 inches. The fibrous roots form a
thick, dense block. The dark green leaves, which may be tinged
with red, are hairy and up to 6 inches long. The flowers, up to
2 inches long, are borne in thick clusters at the top of the stem
from mid- to late summer.

CULTIVATION

Bergamot is best suited to moist soil, or any good garden soil
to which moisture-retentive material has been added, and it
loves to sunbathe. It is quite adaptable to a shaded position
provided its feet remain damp. Chalky soils do not suit it at all
well and it dislikes humid winters because its annual growth
cycle is hindered.

A piece pulled from the outer edges of an established clump
in spring will soon establish itself, and cuttings may be taken
at the same time. The clumps form a mat-like growth and tend
to become bare in the middle, so they need to be broken up
and divided every three or four years.

HOW TO USE

Fresh leaves may be used sparingly in salads, fruit salad, and
fruit drinks, and fresh or dried leaves made into a refreshing
and relaxing tea that is said to be soporific.

The dried leaves lend a pleasantly citrus aroma to potpourri blends.

Myrrhis odorata

SWEET CICELY

A SUCCULENT SALAD OF SWEET CICELY ROOTS LIGHTLY
BOILED AND SERVED WITH A VINAIGRETTE OR CREAMY
DRESSING; A FRUIT SALAD GIVEN THE SLIGHTLY ANISE
FLAVOR OF THE LEAVES; A SUMMER FLOWER
ARRANGEMENT ENHANCED BY THE LONG STEMS OF
FLUFFY CREAM-COLORED FLOWERS . . .

Sweet cicely grows wild in northern Europe, and provides
good visual value in a border or herb garden. With its large,
bright-green, lacy leaves and mass of creamy-white flowers
borne on huge umbel-like clusters, it makes a perfect back-of-
the-border plant, reaching in some cases a height of 6 feet. It
is in full leaf from very early spring until mid-winter, after
most herbs have died back, and is therefore especially useful.
The whole plant of this herbaceous perennial is fragrant, with
a mildly aniseed aroma that complements fruit dishes. The
leaves do not dry well and are best used fresh.

HISTORY

In his *Herball*, Gerard stated that when the seeds were eaten
with oil, vinegar, and pepper they "exceed all other salads".
The botannical name of the plant is thought to recognize that
the leaves have an aroma similar to that of myrrh, and the
popular name indicates its sweet flavor. To this end, in
medieval times it was used in fruit dishes as a sugar substitute.

IDENTIFICATION

The plant is so decorative, neat, and tidy, it easily earns a place
in a flower border, where it may spread to 3 feet across and
grows to twice that height. The thick, hollow stems are deeply
ridged, while the leaves, pale on the undersides, are toothed
and fern-like, and up to 12 inches long. The flowers appear in
late spring and early summer, are attractive to bees, and
number among the prettiest of the umbellifers. The roots are
long, thick, and fleshy, and, like a parsnip, white inside a light
brown skin. The seeds, which may be up to 1 inch long, are
brownish black, long, narrow, and sharply pointed.

CULTIVATION

The long carrot-like roots love a cool moist soil, and given
partial shade the plants will survive for several years. However, it is best to divide them in the fall when the top growth
dies down. Plant out any self-sown seedlings which may
emerge all around the mother plants. Purchased seed should
be sown in the fall.

Sweet cicely is not suitable for growing in humid areas,
because it needs a good dormant period during the winter to
produce its root and lush foliage.

An American woodland plant, *Osmorrhiza longistylis*, known
as smoother sweet cicely, is very similar but has a very slightly
larger leaf. The roots used to be nibbled by children for the
anise/licorice flavor.

Above:
*Sweet cicely, which grows
to a height of 6 feet, blends
well with tall border plants
such as foxgloves and
hollyhocks.*

HOW TO USE

The leaves may be used fresh in salads and fruit salads, and
chopped into other fruit dishes such as pies and compotes.
The peeled roots can be boiled and eaten as a vegetable,
accompanied by a white sauce or vinaigrette dressing. The
seeds are used in the making of Chartreuse liqueur.

Left:
*The bright-green, fern-like
leaves of sweet cicely are
delicious when used in
salads and fruit salads.*

Nepeta cataria

CATNIP

A PLANT OF SPREADING CATNIP IN THE BORDER AS A
COMFORT PATCH FOR THE FELINE POPULATION; A
FEW LEAVES USED CAUTIOUSLY IN SALADS; A TISANE
MADE FROM FRESH OR DRIED LEAVES AND TAKEN
WHEN RELAXATION IS THE ORDER OF THE DAY . . .

Catnip, the herb so attractive to the feline population, has few
culinary uses. With its gently curved spikes of heart-shaped
grey-green leaves and clusters of white or pale blue flowers, it
is, however, an attractive addition to a border.

HISTORY

The plant, a herbaceous perennial, is native to Asia and Europe
and was widely used in self-help medicines. In his *Herball*,
Gerard recommends it for colds, coughs, chest complaints,
and nervousness.

IDENTIFICATION

The plant grows to a height of up to 3 feet, with a spread of 15
inches. It has a straggly habit, and is liable to be squashed flat
by cats rolling on it. Indeed, to preserve plants from this in-
evitable fate, it may be necessary to protect them with wire
netting.

CULTIVATION

Catnip can be grown from seed planted in spring or summer
in good fertile soil in partial shade, or by root division or
cuttings taken in spring.

HOW TO USE

The fresh leaves, which have a very strong aroma, can be used
sparingly in salads.

A tisane made from the leaves and flowers may be taken for
coughs, colds, and catarrh, and is noted as a soothing bedtime
drink.

Right:

*Catnip is distinguished by
the small purple flowers
which form just above the
pairs of leaves at the top of
the long, straight stems.*

Left:

*It is advisable to protect
clumps of catnip by wires
or an enclosing circle of
wire netting to prevent cats
from rolling on them.*

Ocimum basilicum

SWEET BASIL

A GLISTENING TOMATO SALAD MADE ALL THE MORE
PIQUANT AND COLORFUL FOR A SCATTERING OF TORN
BASIL LEAVES; ROAST CHICKEN COOKED WITH A BASIL
AND ORANGE STUFFING . . .

With a pot of basil on the windowsill and a tomato plant in a
window box outside, you have the perfect partnership for
many summer salads, sauces and casseroles, for basil and
tomatoes go together in any combination you care to mention.
The herb is a half-hardy annual emanating from warm climates
and is therefore a sun-lover. With care and adequate heat, a
plant will stay in leaf inside right through to mid-winter, a
luxury for those who love to use their herbs fresh. You can
freeze basil, or preserve it in the Italian way, the leaves packed
into jars with rock salt and olive oil.

HISTORY

Basil traveled overland to Europe via the Middle East from
India, where it is considered sacred by the Hindus. A Belgian
old wives' tale of the 16th century told that basil leaves
crushed between two bricks would turn into scorpions, while
Boccaccio has his heroine Lisabetta burying her lover's head
in a pot of basil and watering it with her tears.

IDENTIFICATION

According to type, a basil plant can have either a multitude of
minute leaves or ones up to 4 inches long and almost half as
wide, glossy, smooth, silky, and highly aromatic – they smell
something like cloves. The stems tend to be woody and
straggly, and the flowers, in long spikes, are small, white, and
tubular. They appear from mid-summer through to the fall.
The plants can reach a height of 2 feet.

CULTIVATION

In zones with a cold winter, sow basil in early to mid-spring in
boxes or in frames, or later outside when all danger of frost
has passed. The best results are obtained by starting off the
seedlings with protection and maintaining a high temperature
until they can be hardened off and planted out safely.

In warmer zones, sow directly into the beds, and thin out to
about 8 inches apart, or transplant. Basil seedlings transplant
easily. A plant can be potted up and kept inside to maintain a
fresh supply of leaves until late fall, or it can be grown inside
where the plant will get at least five hours of sunshine each
day. It is a good patio or window-box plant, and a happy
inhabitant of a sunbaked yard.

HOW TO USE

In Italy and France, basil is used to make, respectively, *pesto*
or *pistou* sauce (see recipe overleaf), in which it is crushed
with garlic and pine kernels. The sauce may be served with
spaghetti or stirred into soup. Basil is good not only with
tomatoes, but with sweet peppers, eggplant, and zucchini;
with chicken, eggs, and steak (when it is pounded with
softened butter and drizzled over the meat).

Medicinally, it may be used as a mild sedative and to relieve
stomach pains and sickness. A pot of basil in the kitchen is
said to discourage flies.

Above:

*Sweet basil, the herb that so
perfectly partners tomato
dishes of all kinds, is
frequently served in pasta
sauces.*

Right:

This patio container has been planted with two distinct varieties of basil, together with some parsley and chives.

PESTO SAUCE

Serves 4

Ingredients
⅓ cup fresh basil leaves
2 cloves garlic, crushed
pinch of salt
½ cup pine kernels
¾ cup parmesan cheese
½ cup olive oil

Preparation

Blend the basil leaves in a liquidizer. If your supply of basil is insufficient, combine fresh parsley and basil for a slightly different flavor.

—

Add the garlic and olive oil and process for a few seconds.

—

Gradually add the pine kernels, Parmesan cheese and season, remembering that Parmesan has a salty taste. The consistency should be thick and creamy.

—

This quantity of pesto is sufficient for 1 pound cooked drained pasta. Mix 2 tablespoons pesto with the pasta and serve on individual plates with an extra spoonful of pesto on each helping.

Origanum majorana

SWEET MARJORAM

ANCHOVIES DRESSED WITH LEMON JUICE, OLIVE OIL AND SWEET MARJORAM LEAVES TO SERVE AS AN APPETIZER; EGGS BAKED UNDER A COVERING OF LIGHT CREAM AND CHOPPED MARJORAM; GRILLED MEATS GENEROUSLY SPRINKLED WITH THE DRIED HERB AND COOKED TO A SIZZLING BROWN . . .

Sweet or knotted marjoram is highly perfumed and has thick trusses of dainty white or purple flowers, which make it one of the most decorative plants in the herb garden. It also represents good value since the leaves dry or freeze well for culinary use, and the flowers may be dried for long-lasting arrangements or pot pourri. In warm climates, where it originates, sweet marjoram is a perennial, but it must be treated as a half-hardy annual in colder conditions, since it will not survive severe winters.

HISTORY

Sweet marjoram has been cultivated since ancient times. It is a native of central Europe, where it was grown for its many medicinal uses.

IDENTIFICATION

The plant grows to about 10 inches high, with a spread of 8 inches. The stems are tough, woody, and inclined to be straggly, while the dark greyish-green leaves are oval and up to ¾ inch long. The flowers are minute but plentiful, and are borne in clusters around the stem. They are produced from green pea-like buds known as "knots," which give the plant its alternative name.

CULTIVATION

Pot or wild marjoram is simple to raise from seed sown in spring or from summer cuttings or from root division in fall. On the other hand sweet marjoram needs to be treated as a half hardy annual. All three kinds can be started by sowing inside or in cold frames early in spring, and are ready to transfer outside as soon as the temperature gets up to about 45°. In very mild zones they can be treated as hardy.

Origanum dictammus, dittany of Crete, is grown as oregano in America, often as a pot plant and usually only for decoration – although its leaves can be added to salads.

HOW TO USE

Add fresh leaves to casseroles just before serving to retain the full flavor. They can also be used in sauces, stuffings, sparingly in salads, in egg and cheese dishes, and in fruit salads.

Medicinally, the plant may be taken as a digestive, and it is useful in the home as an insect repellant.

With their sweet, pungent aroma, the dried leaves and flowers are good in pot pourri and herbal sleep pillows.

Hang the flower stems upside down in a warm, airy place to dry them for arranging.

Left:

Brilliant in the summer sunshine, a clump of low-growing, compact, and yellow-leaved golden marjoram (see previous page.)

Far left:

Oregano, known as rigani *in Greece, dries particularly well and retains its aroma for a long time.*

Left:

Later in the summer, this patch of oregano will be a mass of purple flowers which attract the bees and butterflies.

Origanum vulgare

OREGANO

CALAMARI SOUP RICH WITH TOMATO AND AROMATIC WITH FRESH OREGANO LEAVES; CHICKEN RISOTTO WITH OREGANO STIRRED IN AT THE POINT OF SERVING; EGGPLANT SALAD, *MELITZANESALATA*, SPRINKLED WITH THE FRESH OR DRIED HERB FOR THE UNMISTAKEABLE FLAVOR OF GREECE . . .

Oregano is a very close relative of marjoram, so much so there is some confusion in the cross-pollination of their names: what is known as marjoram in Britain turns up as oregano in Italy! This is the pungently aromatic herb of southern Italy, the one that is used, mainly in its dried form, to flavor pizzas and tomato sauces. Indeed, Greek cooks are convinced that dried oregano – *rigani* – is best used dried and, what's more, is the only herb worth drying!

HISTORY

The plant originates from the Mediterranean region, where its pungency is in direct proportion with its quota of sun. It is a traditional ingredient of Mexican chilli powder, and has long been used as a flavouring for chilli sauces and chilli beans.

IDENTIFICATION

This hardy annual grows to a height of about 8 inches, with woody stems and dark green leaves around ¾ inch long. The flowers, borne on long spikes, are small and white in color.

CULTIVATION

The plant demands a well-drained soil in full sun, though a poor, rocky soil will be adequate. Plant seed in warm soil in late spring, or, in mid-spring, in pots or seed trays under glass. Oregano does especially well in inside mini-propagators placed on the windowsill.

HOW TO USE

The fresh leaves, which are sold in bundles in Italian and Greek markets, are useful additions to salads, casseroles (towards the end of cooking), soups, sauces, pâtés, and poultry dishes. Dried oregano is especially good with tomatoes, beans, eggplant, zucchini, and rice, and in dishes such as pilaf and risotto.

COTTABULLA

Serves 8

Cottabulla, a dish of West Indian origin, is a tasty cross
between a cold meatloaf and a pâté campagne

Ingredients

½ pound stale white bread, crusts removed
2 pounds ground beef
2 medium onions, finely chopped
2 eggs
1 teaspoon ground coriander
1 teaspoon dried oregano
1 tablespoon paprika
3 cloves of garlic, crushed
pinch of cayenne
1 teaspoon sugar
salt and freshly ground black pepper

Oven temperature: 375°

Preparation

Soak the bread in water, squeeze out and crumble. Mix all the
ingredients together thoroughly, seasoning with plenty of salt
and pepper.

—

Pack into a large soufflé dish leaving a slight hollow in the
middle. Cover with foil and bake for 40 to 50 minutes until
cooked through, but still slightly pink in the middle.

—

While it is still hot, put a plate slightly smaller than the baking
dish on top of the foil and weight it with some heavy cans.
Leave until cold and firm, remove the weights and refrigerate
until needed.

—

To serve, slice into wedges. Cottabulla can also be served hot,
in which case there is no need to weight it. Alternatively,
shape the mixture into patties, roll in seasoned flour, and fry,
grill or barbecue to make sensational hamburgers.

Pelargonium

SCENTED-LEAVED GERANIUM

A TRIO OF LEMON-SCENTED LEAVES LINING THE BASE OF A SPONGE CAKE PAN; A SPRAY OR TWO OF THE LEAVES DECORATING A JEWEL-RED ENGLISH SUMMER PUDDING; A FEW NUTMEG-SCENTED LEAVES STREWN INTO THE MILK WHEN MAKING CUSTARD . . .

A pot of scented-leaved geranium in the kitchen is one of the most useful of herbs. You can put a couple of leaves in the base of a cake pan when making sponge cakes or other baked goods, add a leaf or two to sauces, syrups, salads, and fruit salads, and use the pretty, sometimes variegated leaves for decorating and garnishing dishes of all kinds. The pelargonium species originate in South Africa, and are ideal for growing inside. Outside, they are half-hardy perennials that collapse at the first touch of frost. Different varieties have different aromas. You can choose between lemon scented, *P. crispum minor*; apple scented, *P. odoratissimum*; oak-leaf scented, *P. quercifolium*; rose scented, *P. graveolens* and *P. radens*; nutmeg scented, *P. fragrans*; peppermint scented, *P. tomentosum*, and many others. The flowers, which may be white, pink, purple, red, or variegated are small and insignificant, and most, disappointingly, have no smell.

Above:
One of the many varieties of scented geranium, Pelargonium crispum minor smells of lemons.

HISTORY
The plants were "discovered" by Tradescent, the gardener of Charles I of England, and he grew a number of varieties in the royal greenhouses. One of the first to be brought to England was *P. triste*, which numbers among the few species that have scented flowers as well as foliage.

IDENTIFICATION
The plants have dark green, pale green, or green-and-cream variegated leaves, which may be deeply cut or frilled and may vary in size from ½ inch to 3 inches across. The five-petaled flowers are borne in clusters and are long-lived. Height varies considerably, and may be between 1 foot and 3 feet. The stems are tough and woody.

CULTIVATION
Pelargonium are grown from tip cuttings taken under cover in spring and summer. They like a good well-drained soil, plenty of sun, and protection from cold. Grown inside, they require plant food once a week to encourage full leaf growth. The plants should be cut back in winter to avoid their becoming straggly.

Left:
Scented geraniums make lovely border plants, but they are killed by the first frost.

HOW TO USE
The fresh leaves may be infused in milk, cream, and syrups for desserts, sherbets, and ices; chopped into softened butter for sandwiches and cake fillings; and used extensively for garnishing.

The dried leaves are a fragrant addition to potpourri and sachets to scent clothes and linen.

The fresh leaves can be infused in bath water or rinsing water for hair.

Right:

The familiar curled-leaf parsley, which is widely used for garnishing meat, fish and vegetable dishes of all kinds, has a strong, almost sweet flavor.

Far right:

Neapolitan parsley, also known as flat-leaved parsley, has a sharper and more pronounced flavor than the curly-leaved type.

Petroselinum crispum

PARSLEY

ROWS OF FINELY CHOPPED PARSLEY SEPARATING THE LIGHT AND DARK MEATS IN DRESSED CRAB; PARSLEY SAUCE BRINGING OUT THE SUBTLE FLAVOR OF POACHED FISH; PARSLEY AS ONE OF THE CLASSIC *FINES HERBES* TO FLAVOR CHEESE AND EGG DISHES . . . .

Parsley is an invaluable addition to bouquets garnis and *fines herbes* mixtures for grills and fish dishes. With its deep green, frilled or curly leaves, it is one of the best-known and most widely used herbs, as much for garnishing as for cooking. Neapolitan parsley, whose flat leaves are reminiscent of coriander, is less decorative, has a sharper flavor, and is easier to grow.

HISTORY

A native of the eastern Mediterranean region, parsley was first recorded, in a Greek herbal, as long ago as the 3rd century BC. It was used in ancient Rome in cooking and for cerermonial purposes. Pliny recorded that if scattered in a fish pond it had the power to cure unhealthy fish.

IDENTIFICATION

The plant grows to a height of up to 18 inches, with a spread of 10 inches. The stems, which are also strongly aromatic, are green and supple, the leaves curled or flat. The flowers, which appear in the late summer of the plant's second year, are small and a yellowish green color.

CULTIVATION

Originating from the regions around the Black Sea, parsley is best sown in mid- to late spring as an edging in the kitchen or herb garden or even to a flower border. Germination can be unbelievably slow, about six to eight weeks is the norm, but to encourage it try soaking the seed overnight and wetting the drill with water trickled from a kettle of boiling water immediately prior to sowing. (Legend has it that parsley seed goes nine times to the devil and back before germinating.) Subsequently thin the little plants with care during showery weather, or remove alternate plants for use until they are left standing about 12 inches apart.

In all but the most northerly parts of America, parsley should be sown in early spring, or even in fall as long as this is before the ground freezes. Remove the flower stalks as they form to keep the plant buoyant and the leaves full of flavor.

Grow some in a container and keep it in a porch or on the kitchen window-sill for a fresh supply of leaves during the winter months, as parsley does not dry successfully. Although it will freeze, it loses its pert frilliness and is no longer attractive as a garnish.

HOW TO USE

Parsley has its culinary uses in nearly every savory category of food, not only in garnishing but in preparing soups, sauces, and casseroles, in marinades, and with meat, poultry, fish, and vegetables. Often a sprig of parsley – surprisingly hard to come by unless you grow your own – is all that is needed to present a dish attractively.

The plant may be used for kidney complaints, as a tonic, and in the treatment of flatulence.

An infusion splashed on the skin is said to lighten freckles and prevent thread veins.

The leaves also provide a green or yellow dye.

SALSA VERDE

Serves 4

I n g r e d i e n t s
3 cloves of garlic, finely chopped
2 cups parsley, finely chopped
1 tablespoon watercress leaves, finely chopped
(optional)
1 tablespoon mixed fresh herbs, finely chopped (basil, marjoram, and a little thyme, sage, chervil, and dill)
coarse salt
4 tablespoons olive oil
juice of 1–2 lemons
1–2 teaspoons sugar
black pepper

Green and piquant, this sauce of fresh herbs is excellent with any fish and seafood, hot or cold, and also goes well with hard-boiled eggs.

P r e p a r a t i o n
Blend or pound in a mortar the garlic, parsley, watercress, fresh mixed herbs, and a little coarse salt until they form a smooth paste.
—
Add the oil, a spoonful at a time, and mix well. Add the lemon juice and season with sugar, salt and pepper to taste.

Poterium sanguisorba

SALAD BURNET

BURNET VINEGAR, A PIQUANT ADDITION TO THE RANGE OF SALAD DRESSING INGREDIENTS; BURNET BUTTER TO DRIZZLE OVER GRILLED FISH OR MEATS; AND BURNET LEAVES ADDED SPARINGLY, FOR THEIR BITTER-SWEETNESS, TO MIXED GREEN SALADS . . .

A popular herb in English cottage gardens, salad burnet was taken to North America by the early colonists. It is native to Europe, where it grows on chalky soil, and particularly on the chalk downs of southern England. With their mild, cucumber-like flavor, the young leaves are useful in salads and, like borage, in ice-cold summer drinks. It is now mainly used in France and Italy, where it is frequently included in bunches of mixed salad leaves and herbs sold in markets.

HISTORY
Salad burnet, or lesser burnet (previously *Sanguisorba minor*), was a favorite salad herb in Elizabethan times, when the soft, blue-green leaves were prized for their "cool," mild flavor.

IDENTIFICATION
The plant grows to a height of about 16 inches, with a spread of 9 inches. The small, heavily toothed, blue-green leaves are carried in pairs, widely spaced along the slender, curving stems. The red flowers, which appear in early summer, form small, spherical heads about ½ inch across.

CULTIVATION
The plant, a herbaceous perennial, likes a chalky well-drained soil and a sunny, sheltered position. It can be grown from seed planted in spring, or by root division in fall. The leaves last well into winter and appear again in early spring, so it is virtually evergreen.

HOW TO USE
Fresh leaves may be used in salads, sauces, soups, and pâtés; in softened butter known as *ravigote*; steeped in vinegar for salad dressing; as a garnish; and in fruit salads and drinks.

Medicinally, the fresh leaves act as a digestive. In self-help medicine, a decoction of the roots was used to stop bleeding, and an infusion of the leaves to cool sunburn.

Right:
Salad burnet plants are thick and bushy and tightly compact, their tiny red flowers towering above the leaves on long, slender stalks.

Rosmarinus officinalis

ROSEMARY

ROAST LAMB WITH A GENEROUS SPRIG OF ROSEMARY
PRESSED CLOSE AGAINST THE SIZZLING SKIN;
CHOPPED ROSEMARY IN COUNTRY-STYLE SAUSAGES,
GIVING THEM THE FLAVOR OF ITALY; SOOTHING
ROSEMARY TEA, TAKEN ICE-COLD WITH LEMON AND
HONEY . . .

An evergreen shrub, rosemary is available fresh year-round.
This is just as well because, once dried, it loses much of its
flavor, and its pine-needle-like leaves become unpalatably
spiky. It is a pretty herb, with trusses of pale or bright blue
flowers lasting, in the right climate, right through spring and
summer. It is native to the countries bordering the Mediterranean, where it grows in profusion, its slightly camphoric
scent far more pronounced than it can ever be in cooler
climatic conditions.

Left:
A sprig of rosemary is the
perfect addition to roast or
grilled lamb as well as
being an attractive herb.

Far left:
Rosemary, which grows
into a thick, dense bush,
likes a light, well-drained
soil and a sheltered
position.

CHICKPEA SOUP

Serves 4–6

I n g r e d i e n t s

4 cloves of garlic
½ teaspoon dried or 1 teaspoon fresh rosemary
4 tablespoons olive oil
5-ounce can plum tomatoes
1 pound can chickpea, drained and rinsed
1 chicken bouillon cube
2 cups water
salt and pepper to taste

P r e p a r a t i o n

Peel and crush the garlic. If using fresh rosemary, chop it very finely.

—

Heat the oil and sauté the garlic until it begins to brown. Add the rosemary and the tomatoes, roughly chopped, and lower the heat to a simmer when the ingredients come to the boil. Cook for 25 minutes or so.

—

When the tomatoes are cooked, add the chickpeas and cook a further 5 minutes.

—

Stir in the bouillon cube and no more than 2 cups water. Season with salt and pepper to taste and serve.

HISTORY

The name means dew (*ros*) of the sea (*marinus*) – the sea being the Mediterranean. In the Middle Ages in Britain, sprigs of rosemary were dipped in gold and tied with ribbon as a keepsake for wedding guests, and the herb was a traditional gift on New Year's day. Shakespeare immortalized its significance in the age-old language of flowers when Hamlet tells Ophelia, "There's rosemary, that's for remembrance."

IDENTIFICATION

In the proper conditions, the bush can grow to a height of 6½ feet and spread 5 feet across. The leaves are dark green on top and silver-grey on the underside, about 1 inch long and ⅛ inch wide. The two-lipped tubular flowers are small, about ½ inch long, and carried on long thick spikes. The stems become tough and woody.

CULTIVATION

Take cuttings of the twisted wood of non-flowering shoots in early summer, or layer established branches in summer. Choose a sheltered position and well drained soil in which to plant it so that it can sunbathe. Where winters are cold, grow rosemary in containers that can be taken into shelter. The thick growth tolerates clipping, so it can be controlled.

HOW TO USE

Rosemary and lamb go together in many ways. Make slits in lamb for roasting and tuck in sprigs of the herb, place larger sprigs over chops for grilling, and include them in casseroles and stews. Use rosemary in bouquets garnis, sparingly with fish, and in rice dishes.

Medicinally, a tisane of the leaves is taken as a tonic for calming nerves, and is also used as an antiseptic.

Use an infusion, too, as a rinse to lighten blond hair.

The dried leaves are used in potpourri and, in sachets, to scent clothes and linen.

Rumex scutanus

SORREL

SORREL LEAVES GENTLY TORN AND SERVED AS A PIQUANT GREEN SALAD WITH A BUILT-IN FLAVOR; THE LEAVES COOKED AS SPINACH, DRAINED THOROUGHLY AND SPRINKLED WITH LEMON JUICE; OR LIGHTLY COOKED TO FLOAT IN A CLEAR BROTH IN THE SPANISH STYLE . . .

French sorrel, as it is sometimes known, is similar to spinach with lemony overtones, and so makes a distinctive and useful herb and vegetable. A herbaceous perennial, it is easy to grow, is always on hand, and has a variety of uses. And with its green-tipped-with-red flower spikes, it is decorative, too. In short, it earns its keep in any decorative or kitchen border.

HISTORY

Sorrel was used as a herb and vegetable in ancient Egypt, while the Greeks and Romans knew it, too, as an antidote to rich foods and fatty meats. It was popular in Britain during the Middle Ages, where it had both culinary and medicinal uses. A native of Europe and Asia, it was brought to England by the Romans and to America by the pilgrims.

IDENTIFICATION

French Sorrel can reach a height of 2 feet and a spread of 9 inches, though it is best used young, before it is fully matured and the long flower spikes form. The spinach-like leaves are deep dark green and shield shaped; they may be up to 6 inches long and 3 inches across. The flowers, which appear in late spring, are small, greenish-red, and, like dock – to which French sorrel is related – they are borne on tall, majestic, loosely formed spikes.

CULTIVATION

Raise new plants each season for the most refined flavor, sowing seed in spring in moist well-nourished soil where there is some shade during the day. Set in drills as for most salad crops; thin the little plants to about 12 inches apart. Prevent bolting by removing flower buds and pick the leaves frequently to maintain a supply of fresh succulent leaves.

Pinch out the flower heads to prevent flowering and seeding, or else be prepared to remove self-sown seedlings before they develop. Once sorrel establishes itself, the roots plunge deeply and are difficult to eradicate. In really warm summers, or generally warm regions, French sorrel leaves tend to become bitter. A mulch around the plants will help to keep the soil cooler, but once the season cools down the leaf flavor will improve.

HOW TO USE

The leaves may be cooked as a vegetable, drained well, and dressed with oil and vinegar, cream, yogurt, or a dash of lemon juice. They are very good as salad, and make an unusual and delicious soup garnished with swirls of cream and garlic croûtons. They are also used in lamb and beef casseroles, and to curdle milk and make junket.

POACHED SALMON WITH SORREL SAUCE

Serves 4

I n g r e d i e n t s

4 cutlets of salmon
½ cup sweet butter
1 large bunch of sorrel, washed and chopped
1 cup heavy cream or crème fraîche
salt and pepper

P r e p a r a t i o n

Poach the salmon in boiling salted water for about 8 minutes. Remove and set aside on a warm plate.

—

Melt the butter in a saucepan. Add the chopped sorrel – it melts into the butter very quickly. When it has bubbled for a few minutes, add the cream and seasoning, bring to the boil and simmer for 10 minutes. If you are using crème fraîche, boil very rapidly for a few minutes.

—

Pour the sauce over the salmon and serve immediately.

Above:
For a more abundant crop of sorrel leaves, cut off the flower heads. You can dry them for decorative use.

Ruta graveolens

RUE

THE COMPACT, TIGHTLY GROWING PLANTS CLIPPED
TO MAKE AN ATTRACTIVE EDGING IN A HERB GARDEN;
THE DRIED SEEDHEADS SPRAYED GOLD FOR A
SPARKLING HRISTMAS DECORATION; OR USED IN
THEIR NATURAL STATE, CHESTNUT BROWN AND SHINY,
IN DRIED FLOWER ARRANGEMENTS. . . .

Most herbs have retained their popularity over the centuries
not only because of their culinary and medicinal properties,
but also their pleasant scent. That cannot be said of rue, a herb
whose aroma has been likened, not unfairly, to the smell of
tom cats. Accordingly, its culinary applications have not been
enthusiastically handed down from one generation to the
next, while even its medicinal applications need approaching
with care.

Rue, a sub-shrub known as the herb of grace, is a native of
southern Europe, where it will flourish in the poorest of soils.
It will easily take to poor garden soil, as well, where it makes a
compact and decorative bush.

HISTORY

The ancient Greeks credited rue with the ability to improve
eyesight, and, in his *Herball,* Gerard took up this theme,
recommending it to be boiled, pickled, and eaten "to quicken
the sight."

IDENTIFICATION

The bush can grow to 2½ feet tall, with a width of 18 inches.
The stems are tough and woody, while the bluish-green leaves
are pointed oval, and deeply divided. The flowers are bright
yellow and have four petals, about ½ inch across, borne in
loose clusters. The seedheads are chestnut brown, and look
rather like miniature wood carvings.

CULTIVATION

Raised from seed sown in spring and thinned out to about 18
inches apart, rue can make a good herb garden hedge and its
evergreen nature lends itself to this use. Cuttings taken in
summer will strike quite easily. Rue revels in a well-drained
soil and loves a sunny, sheltered site. It benefits from being
cut back in the spring to encourage new fresh growth.

HOW TO USE

The plant is not now used in the kitchen, and should be
approached with extreme care for medicinal purposes. The
tisane – which was once taken for rheumatism, and used,
much diluted, as an eye bath – is not now recommended.
Sprays of the leaves may be hung inside to repel insects.

The seedheads are particularly attractive, and can be used
in dried flower arrangements.

Above:
*Rue leaves have a strong,
bitter aroma and an
unpleasantly astringent
taste. They may be used
inside to repel insects.*

Below:
*Rue has decorative yellow
flowers which are seen to
good advantage against the
grey-green leaves. Later in
the season it carries
attractive brown seedpods.*

Salvia officinalis

SAGE

FRESH SAGE LEAVES LIGHTLY FRIED IN OIL OR BUTTER TO SERVE WITH VEAL ESCALOPE; SAGE AND ONION STUFFING FOR THE CHRISTMAS GOOSE OR A ROAST OF PORK; DRIED PURPLE SAGE LEAVES, AN EVERGREEN ADDITION TO A DRIED FLOWER COLLECTION . . .

Sage is a decorative evergreen sub-shrub, though its leaves are not necessarily green. Some varieties have grey or grey-green downy leaves, and one has deep purple leaves and exceptionally pretty purple-blue flowers. The flavor, which has faint overtones of camphor, is very strong in some types, so making sage a herb to use little and often. The plant is a native of the Mediterranean region, where it thrives on poor, dry soil.

HISTORY

Sage, which takes its name from the Latin *salvere*, "to save," has a long history as a medicinal plant and was listed as such in Theophratus' works. It was much in evidence in Roman times, again for medicinal purposes, but was well established mainly as a culinary herb in medieval England.

IDENTIFICATION

The plant can reach a height of 2 feet, with a spread of 18 inches. The stems are tough and woody, and the leaves, elongated ovals, can be 2½ inches long and ¾ inch across. The flowers, which appear in mid-summer, are about 1 inch long, borne on long, curving clusters.

CULTIVATION

Select a sunny corner and alkaline soil for sage is a native of the Mediterranean shores and flourishes best when it is warm. Propagation is from summer cuttings taken with a heel or by layering established branches in spring and fall. Seed is unreliable and it rarely sets in Britain because sage is reluctant to flower. Where seed is available it is a slow and challenging method of perpetuating the plants. Keep the bushy plants well pruned to encourage young shoots with a strong flavor and because sage has a strong tendency to become leggy and twiggy.

HOW TO USE

Sage is traditionally used in sauces and stuffings for fatty meats such as goose, duck, and pork, in bouquets garnis, and in sausages. In Italy, the fresh leaves are lightly fried with liver, and rolled up with ham and veal in *saltimbocca*. In Germany and Belgium, they are added to eel and other oily fish dishes, while in Middle Eastern countries they are liberally used in salads.

Medicinally, the leaves are used as an antiseptic and an astringent, while the tea is taken for sore throats and to calm the nerves.

Sage leaves are strewn in bath water, and in the rinsing water when washing hair to strengthen dark coloring.

Dark sage leaves are a frequent potpourri ingredient.

ROAST STUFFED PORK STEAK

Serves 6

Ingredients

4 tablespoons butter
1 onion, finely chopped
2 large tart apples
1 handful of fresh sage and thyme, chopped
salt and pepper
2 pounds cooked mashed potato
2 pounds pork steak or fillet
2 tablespoons butter
2 tablespoons water or cider

Oven temperature: 350°

The classic marriage of pork and sage, cooked to a traditional Irish recipe.

Preparation

Make the stuffing first. Add the butter, chopped onion, chopped apple, herbs, salt and pepper to the mashed potato. Mix well and check the seasoning.

—

Place the meat in a ring shape in a casserole or roasting pan. Put the stuffing in the middle. Rub the meat with salt and butter and put a little water or cider in the pan, cover loosely with foil and cook in the oven for about 1 hour.

—

Serve hot with the reduced pan juices, or cold, with roasted apples.

Right:

Clary, with its thick, rounded leaves and paper bracts, is a close relation of sage. Its name is derived from the folkloric term, clear eye.

Far right:

With its stout, sturdy stems and reaching a height of 3 feet, clary is a vigorous plant which looks well in a herbaceous border.

HISTORY

A sixteenth century botanist said of clary that "it restores the natural heat, and comforts the vital spirits, and helps the memory." At the same time, the leaves were used in omelets, and made into fritters to serve with orange or lemon juice.

IDENTIFICATION

Clary grows to a height of 3 feet, with a spread of about 12 inches. It has oval, downy, dark green leaves, which can be up to 8 inches long. The flower bracts, about 2 inches long, may be purple, pink, or white, and are carried on straight, branching spikes at the top of the plant; the bracts are purple or pink. The fragrance is somewhat balsamic, the taste bitter.

CULTIVATION

The plant is grown from seed planted in spring, and will flower the following year. It requires a light soil and a warm, sheltered position if it is to survive the rigors of winter.

HOW TO USE

The strongly aromatic leaves can be added sparingly in the preparation of soups, casseroles, homemade wines and beer, or made into fritters.

Medicinally, they may be used to make a gargle or mouthwash, and a skin cleanser. Clary's derived name, clear eye, suggests it was also used to concoct an eye bath.

Salvia sclarea

CLARY

USED WITH ELDERFLOWERS IN WINEMAKING TO GIVE IT THE FLAVOR OF MUSCATEL; THE FRESH LEAVES USED SPARINGLY IN ROBUST SOUPS AND, IN THE MEDIEVAL WAY, IN LIGHT FRITTERS TO SERVE WITH A SPRINKLING OF SUGAR . . .

A native of southern Europe, clary was introduced into Britain in the sixteenth century, when it was used in brewing and combined with elderflowers to give wine the flavor of muscatel. It is a close relation of sage and a decorative biennial that is usually treated as an annual.

Sambucus nigra

E L D E R

TRUSSES OF FLUFFY CREAM FLOWERS USED TO MAKE A
COUNTRY-STYLE NON-ALCOHOLIC "CHAMPAGNE," OR
A SPARKLING WINE, OR STREWN WITH BERRIES TO
ENHANCE THE FLAVOR OF PIES, CUSTARDS, AND
FOOLS; THE SUCCULENT BLACK BERRIES USED FOR
WINE OR, WITH APPLES, A HEDGEROW JELLY . . .

In springtime, the aroma of the umbrella-like trusses of
creamy-white elderflowers scents the hedgerows and country
lanes of Britain with a sweet aroma one longs to capture. The
plant is common throughout Europe, western Asia, and North
America, where a related species, *S. canadensis*, American
elder, was used as a folk medicine by the American Indians.

HISTORY
European elder has attracted a strong folk history. It was
thought that a tree planted outside a house kept witches at bay
and protected the house from lightning. Cutting it back was
said to bring bad luck.

ELDERFLOWER "CHAMPAGNE"

Yields 1 gallon

Ingredients
1 gallon water
1½ pounds sugarloaf
1 juicy lemon
4 large elderflower heads
2 tablespoons white wine vinegar

Serve the champagne chilled as a fragrant, refreshing summer
drink.

Preparation
Warm a little of the water, then stir in the sugar until it has
dissolved. Leave to cool. Squeeze the juice from the lemon,
then cut the peel into 4 pieces, discarding the pith.

—

Put the flowers into a large, non-metallic container, add the
pieces of lemon peel, the sweetened water, remaining water
and the vinegar. Stir, then cover and leave for 4–5 days.

—

Strain off the liquid and pour into clean screw-top bottles.
Leave for 6 days, by which time it should be effervescent. If it
is not, leave for up to another 4 days.

IDENTIFICATION
The tree can grow to a height of about 30 feet or more, with a
spread of 9 feet, but many trees are much smaller. The leaves
are dull dark green, about 4 inches long and finely toothed.
The flowers are minute, highly fragrant, and carried in umbel-
like clusters. The purplish-black berries are small and round,
and hang in heavy trusses.

CULTIVATION
The trees like a moist soil and plenty of sun if the flowers are
to develop their maximum fragrance. Elders are grown from
hardwood cuttings taken outside in the fall.

HOW TO USE
Elder flowers are traditionally used to flavor fruit compotes,
salads, and jellies. The berries – usually blended with apples –
can be made into jelly, and other preserves, while both flowers
and berries create excellent wines. The flowers, blended with
lemon and sugar, are used to flavor summer drinks and
cordials. Elderberry soup (again, mixed with apples) is a
popular Scandinavian dish.

Elderflower water is widely used, and sold commercially, as
a skin toner and lightener.

Above:
*Elderflowers are used
to make wine and non-
alcoholic summer drinks,
and to flavor syrups,
sweet sauces and creams.
They have a special affinity
with gooseberries.*

Left:
Elderflower's umbrella-like trusses of minute cream flowers are pleasantly aromatic, and scent the hedgerows in late spring.

Satureja hortensis

SUMMER SAVORY

S. montana

WINTER SAVORY

THE FIRST OF THE YOUNG AND TENDER BROAD BEANS
SPRINKLED WITH THE FIRST OF THE YOUNG AND
TENDER SUMMER SAVORY LEAVES; THE LEAVES OF
WINTER SAVORY ADDED TO A BOUQUET GARNI TO USE
IN MEAT OR VEGETABLE CASSEROLES . . .

Summer savory, a half-hardy annual that self-sows freely, has a strong, hot, and slightly bitter flavor reminiscent of thyme, and retains a particular affinity with peas and beans, broad beans especially.

Winter savory is a shrubby perennial with a similar, though somewhat stronger, flavor that was at one time frequently used with trout and other oily fish.

HISTORY

Both types of herb originate from the Mediterranean region and were much in demand by the Romans, who introduced them to Britain. Savory was said to be a stimulant and, as such, is thought to be an effective aphrodisiac.

IDENTIFICATION

Summer savory grows to a height of 18 inches and 6 inches across. It has an untidy, straggling habit. The leaves are long, narrow, and dark green, rather like soft pine needles. Its flowers are small, pale purple, and insignificant, and bloom well into the fall. Winter savory grows to a height of some 12 inches, and has a spread of around 8 inches. The leaves are greyish green and similar to those of summer savory, while the flowers, borne in spiky clusters, are pinky white or pink.

CULTIVATION

Sow summer savory seed in spring in drills, and thin the little plants to about 6 inches apart. Propagated winter savory from cuttings taken in spring may be divided at any time and the same applies to roots.

Seed can be tried, but it is annoyingly slow to germinate and does not always produce alert-looking seedlings. Both need their share of sunlight and good drainage, as do all plants that come from the Mediterranean. As such, they are very useful for rock gardens and dry banks.

Winter savory can be grown in boxes or containers and can then be brought inside for protection during the winter, or even kept inside where the shoots need to be constantly pinched back to prevent it from becoming leggy and scrawny. It certainly needs good light during the winter when grown in this way.

HOW TO USE

Summer savory is used with pork and game, in soups, sausages, pâtés, and stuffings, in bouquets garnis, and with vegetables, particularly fresh and dried peas and beans. Winter savory has similar uses, but its stronger flavor is considered inferior.

Both herbs may be used as a tonic and a digestive, and are said to ease insect bites and stings.

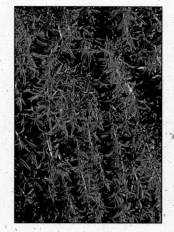

Above:
Winter savory with its slender, pine-needle-like leaves, enjoys a poor soil and a sunny position.

Left:
The leaves of winter savory may be used sparingly with vegetables, especially with peas and beans. The tisane is said to be both a tonic and a digestive.

Symphytum officinale

COMFREY

THE VERY YOUNG LEAVES CHOPPED AND STIRRED INTO
CREAM CHEESE FOR SANDWICHES OR LIGHTLY
COOKED, TOSSED IN MELTED BUTTER AND EATEN AS A
VEGETABLE; THE ROOTS USED AS A FLAVORING FOR A
RANGE OF COUNTRY WINES . . .

Its somewhat comforting name points to the fact that, in
medieval times, comfrey had so many self-help medicinal
applications it was looked upon almost as a cure-all. Its popular
country name, knit-bone, describes one of them: when the
ground root was moistened and applied to a broken joint, the
resulting composition set like plaster.

Comfrey is a native of Asia and Europe and it grows freely in
temperate regions of North America. Indeed, it grows freely
wherever it grows at all, attaining rampant weed proportions
if not contained.

Above:
*The trusses of purple-pink
flowers which last
throughout the summer
compensate for the dense
green lack-luster leaves of
the comfrey plant.*

Right:
*Comfrey plants are
energetic colonizers, and
one piece of root will soon
develop into a large patch.*

HISTORY

The roots and leaves were applied to swellings, sprains,
bruises, and cuts, and as a poultice. They act as soothants for
abscesses, boils, and stings.

IDENTIFICATION

The plant, a perennial, has dull, dark green, hairy leaves,
which may be up to 8 inches long; they have no aroma, and
are not in the least attractive. The bell-shaped flowers are
cream flashed with red, and hang in clusters. The roots are
thick, tapering, and persistently multiply. The plant grows to 3
feet tall, with a spread of 18 inches.

CULTIVATION

When grown from seed, the plants are slow to reach maturity.
More reliable plants are obtained by root division in spring.
Select moisture-retentive soil, or even a poorly drained
corner, and comfrey will thrive for many years. Plants have
been known to span a generation.

Comfrey thrives happily in all but the very coldest regions
where it can be propagated by root cuttings.

HOW TO USE

Comfrey is related to borage, and can be used in similar ways.
The young leaves can be cooked and eaten as spinach.

A cleansing skin oil may be made by steeping young leaves
in good-quality oil, such as almond oil.

The leaves and stalks produce a pale yellow dye.

Right:
*With its bright-green leaves
and large clusters of golden
yellow flowers, tansy (see
overleaf) makes a colorful
impact in a herbaceous
border.*

HOW TO USE

The use of tansy leaves in desserts was once so wide-spread that "tansy" became the generic name for baked or boiled egg custard flavored by infusing the leaves. It may be used in salads, egg dishes, and casseroles, but only in small quantities.

In self-help medicine, the leaves were used as a digestive.

The flowers may be hung in a dry, airy place and used in dried flower arrangements. The dried leaves act as a powerful insect repellant, and were "put up in bags" for this purpose.

Note, the herb should not be taken during pregnancy.

Tanacetum vulgare

TANSY

BUNCHES OF THE SMALL GOLDEN-BALL FLOWERS HANGING DECORATIVELY IN ROOM CORNERS TO DRY OR PROVIDING THE COLORFUL FOCAL POINT IN DRIED FLOWER ARRANGEMENTS; AND THE FLOWER NAME GIVEN TO THE MEDIEVAL DISHES OF CREAMS, CUSTARDS, AND POSSETS . . .

Tansy is a native of Europe and also grows wild in the eastern United States, where it is cultivated commercially. It was a common cottage-garden herb in medieval times, when it was used as an insect repellant, a strewing herb, and as a source of orange dye.

Above:

Tansy leaves have a strong, pungent aroma. Use Tanacetum vulgare *only – and sparingly – in cooking; it should not be taken at all during pregnancy. The flowers dry well and are attractive in long-lasting arrangements.*

HISTORY

During the Middle Ages, the strong, bitter, and some say unpleasant, flavor of the leaves was no barrier to the herb's use in salads, desserts, and cakes, while tansy pancakes, which included thyme, marjoram, and parsley, were a traditional feasting dish at Eastertime.

IDENTIFICATION

A large but graceful plant, tansy can grow to 3 feet tall, with a spread of some 2 feet. It has dark green pinnate leaves about 6 inches long, and umbel-like clusters of small, dome-shaped flowers, bright, deep yellow, and very attractive.

CULTIVATION

The plant is a herbaceous perennial, grown by root division in spring or fall, or from seed sown in spring. It likes a dry, well-drained soil and a sunny outside position.

TANSY & BEEF CASSEROLE

Serves 6

Ingredients

3 tablespoons oil
2 pounds braising steak, cut into ½ inch cubes
6 ounces bacon, diced
2 large onions, finely chopped
1 clove of garlic, crushed
3 large tomatoes, peeled, seeds removed and chopped
1½ cups beef stock
1½ cups red wine
3–4 tablespoons finely chopped tansy (use *Tanacetum vulgare* only – not to be taken during pregnancy)
salt and freshly ground black pepper

Oven temperature: 300°

Preparation

Heat 2 tablespoons oil in a heavy ovenproof casserole, add the beef and bacon in batches, and cook over a moderately high heat, stirring occasionally, until evenly browned. Remove each batch using a slotted spoon and drain on paper towels.

When all the meat has cooked, add the remaining oil to the pan then stir in the onions, garlic, and tomatoes, and cook over a low heat, stirring occasionally, until the onion is soft.

Return the meat to the pan, stir in the stock and wine and bring to simmering point. Add the tansy, salt, and plenty of black pepper. Cover the casserole tightly (use foil if the cover is not a close fit), and place in the oven for about 2 hours, stirring occasionally, until the meat is very tender.

Strain off the liquid and boil until reduced to about 1¼–1½ cups. Keep the meat warm while the liquid is being boiled. Check the seasoning then return the meat for a minute or two. Serve with some tansy sprinkled over the top.

Important: Use *Tanacetum vulgare* only – not to be taken in pregnancy.

Taraxacum officinale

DANDELION

THE BRIGHT GREEN YOUNG LEAVES AS TENDER AS CAN
BE FOR A SALAD OR, LIGHTLY COOKED, AS A
VEGETABLE; THE FLOWERS USED TO MAKE A DRY LIGHT
WINE, TO A GENERATIONS-OLD COUNTRY RECIPE . . .

Dandelion, native to Europe and Asia, is a herbaceous perennial that has become a rampant weed, its bright yellow flowers intruding on many a lawn and well-tended flower border. Its common name comes from the French *dent de lion*, "lion's tooth," signifying the toothed appearance of the leaves. Its more colloquial names – piss-a-beds in English, *pis-en-lit* in French – bear witness to its strong diuretic properties.

HISTORY
In medieval times, dandelion was used as a mild laxative, a diuretic, a tonic, and in the treatment of liver complaints.

IDENTIFICATION
The plant has a persistent root system that, for those who do not appreciate the plant's qualities, is difficult to eradicate. The plant reaches a height of 12 inches. The leaves, which may be up to 8 inches long and 2 inches across, are bright, sharp lettuce green, attractive, and appetizing in appearance. The flowers bloom eight or nine months of the year, are made up of a mass of florets, and measure about 1½ inches across. The seeds form a fluffy ball, known as a clock, which used to be the subject of a children's chanting game.

CULTIVATION
More people are interested in how to eliminate dandelions than to grow them. All you need is the smallest piece of root generously donated by a neighbor, and you will have dandelions for ever.

HOW TO USE
The young leaves, high in vitamins and minerals, make an excellent salad, delicious with a slightly lemony dressing. They may also be lightly cooked like spinach, when they are good served with vinaigrette. The leaves and root are used to give a bitter flavor to country beers such as nettle and burdock. Both the flowers and leaves are used, separately, to make wines.

Dandelion is valued as a medicinal herb for all urinary troubles.

The roots produce a yellow or crimson dye, according to the mordant used.

Left:
*Common dandelion leaves,
flower and seedhead, or
"clock," a familiar sight in
meadows, waysides and –
usually as an unwelcome
guest – in gardens.*

Left:

The tiny purple thyme flowers have a stronger, sweeter aroma than the leaves and can be widely used in cooking.

Thymus vulgaris

GARDEN THYME

CREAMY GOLDEN THYME SAUCE WITH FISH; GARDEN THYME OIL FOR SALAD DRESSINGS; FRAGRANT LEMON THYME LEAVES STREWN IN CUSTARDS AND CREAMS . . .

Thyme is a sun-loving herb, at its aromatic best when growing wild on the sun-baked hills around the Mediterranean. Grown in the garden in less favorable climates, it will be aromatic, but less powerfully so. It is a decorative herb, covered for two or three of the summer months with delicate pale purple flowers, themselves highly fragrant, attractive to bees, and with many culinary uses. Different species offer a range of flavors; try *T. citriodorus*, lemon thyme, for a distinctly citrus aroma, and *T. herba-barona*, caraway thyme, for a spicy flavor. The English wild thyme referred to by Shakespeare is *T. drucei*.

HISTORY
Thyme is one of the oldest recorded culinary herbs, probably in use well before the time of the ancient Greeks. The Romans took it to Britain as part of their culinary armory. In his herbal, Nicholas Culpeper credits it with a singular usefulness; "An infusion of the leaves," he has written, "removes the headache occasioned by inebriation."

IDENTIFICATION
Thyme is a low-growing sub-shrub that can become untidily woody and straggly. It can reach a height and spread of about 8 inches. The leaves are very small, only about ¼ inch long; according to type, they may be green, grey green, yellow, or variegated. The flowers, which cover the plant from early summer, are borne in clusters at the tips of the shoots.

CULTIVATION
Choose the sunniest part of the garden where the soil is well drained or even dry, and a little limy. Most plants will be either short-lived or need some protection from the cold and dampness in winter. In the drier and warmer maritime regions where winter temperatures do not fall too low or too quickly, it is always worth trying to keep thyme. It is a good plant for troughs and containers which can be brought inside during the winter for protection.

Propagation is from seed sown in spring, and the tiny plants put out once they are big enough to handle at about 2 inch intervals. Otherwise, take tip cuttings in summer before flowering starts.

HOW TO USE
Thyme is traditionally used with parsley in stuffings for chicken and pork, and, with the addition of a bay leaf in bouquets garnis for use in soups and casseroles. It is especially good with oil and wine or vinegar in marinades for meat and fish, and with vegetables such as zucchini, eggplant, bell peppers, and tomatoes. It both dries and freezes well, so no kitchen need ever be without it. Lemon thyme may be used in custards, fruit salads, and syrups.

The essential oil – thymol – is a strong antiseptic. Thus an infusion may be used as a mouthwash, a gargle, and a wash for cuts and abrasions.

The dried leaves, especially those of lemon thyme, are used to scent linen, and are an important ingredient in potpourri, herb, and sleep pillows.

Right:

A patch of several varieties of thyme shows how varied and attractive this versatile herb can be.

BEEF BRAISED IN BAROLO

Serves 6

I n g r e d i e n t s

2 tablespoons olive oil
1 beef joint of about 2 pounds
½ cup *tritto* (finely diced vegetables – onions, carrots,
celery – mixed with herbs and steeped in olive oil for at
least 12 hours)
1 cup Barolo or other dry red wine
½ cup fresh or canned plum tomatoes
1 teaspoon each of thyme and marjoram
salt to taste

Oven temperature: 350°

P r e p a r a t i o n

Preheat the oven. Heat the oil over a medium flame and brown
the joint of beef. Seal it on all sides, then set aside.

—

Now add the *tritto* to the beef pan and cook it until soft, 3–4
minutes.

—

Transfer the beef to a casserole a little larger than the beef
itself. Retrieve the *tritto* with a slotted spoon – without the oil.
Spread it over and around the beef. Pour in the wine, the stock,
and the tomatoes; add the herbs.

—

Put the beef in the oven, covered with a well-fitting top. Turn
the joint completely over at half time. Check the liquid
content from time to time; add more water if necessary. If by
the end of the cooking time the sauce is too thin, thicken it by
means of reducing.

—

To serve, carve the joint and spoon the sauce over, checking
for salt before you do.

Trigonella foenum-graecum

FENUGREEK

THE GREEN LEAVES CURRIED AS A SPICY AND PIQUANT
VEGETABLE; THE SEEDS ROASTED AND POUNDED AS A
CURRY SPICE OR, STRAIGHT FROM THE PLANT,
SPROUTED AND EATEN AT THE TWO-LEAF STAGE AS A
HOT AND TASTY SALAD . . .

Fenugreek, which takes its name from the Latin for Greek hay,
has been grown as an animal fodder crop around the Mediterranean region since ancient times. But it is much more valuable and versatile than that. The sprouting seeds may be eaten
at the cotyledon stage as a spicy salad; the fully developed
leaves, too bitter to cook as spinach, are served in the Indian
way, as a curry; and the lightly roasted seeds are used as a
spice, also principally in curries. The ground seeds, containing
coumarin, are a major ingredient in commercially prepared
curry powders.

HISTORY
The plant is a native of western Asia and has been widely
grown in countries bordering the Mediterranean, particularly
in Egypt. Its cultivation in northern Europe was principally
intended for forage, to mix with hay crops.

Below and right:
*The fenugreek plant grows
to a height of 2 feet. The
spicy and pungent seeds are
used in curries and may be
sprouted, when the leaves
are eaten as a salad.*

IDENTIFICATION
The plant, a half-hardy annual, bears some resemblance to
lucerne. It grows to a height of 2 feet, with a spread of 8
inches. The leaves are trefoil, rather like clover, and the
flowers, which appear in late spring, are cream or pale yellow
and vetch-like. The seed is compact and pale brown. Light
roasting brings out the full flavor.

CULTIVATION
The seed may be sown inside in mid-spring or outside in
warm soil in late spring. Fenugreek likes a good, well-drained
soil and a position in full sun, which is essential if the seed is
to set.

HOW TO USE
The sprouted seeds are good as a salad, tossed in a vinaigrette
dressing. The roasted seeds are used in Middle Eastern variations of *halva*, a rich sweetmeat, as well as in curries.

Medicinally, an infusion of the seeds may be taken for
flatulence.

The seed produces a yellow dye.

Urtica dioica

NETTLE

TALL, UNGAINLY NETTLE PLANTS A HAVEN FOR BUTTERFLIES AND MOTHS; THE YOUNG, TENDER LEAVES MADE INTO A NUTRITIOUS AND TASTY SOUP TO SWIRL WITH CREAM OR COOKED, AS SPINACH, TO SERVE WITH A TWIST OF LEMON . . .

The main excuse of many a gardener who has not cleared a patch of stinging nettles is that he has left them for the butterflies and moths, who feed on them voraciously. And the main excuse of many a cook who leaves an unsightly cluster of nettles is that he likes them in soup.

HISTORY

It is said that the Roman soldiers tolerated stinging nettles to keep them warm during long marches in their northern territories.

IDENTIFICATION

The plants, herbaceous perennials, can grow to a dreary-looking 6 feet tall, with a spread of 12 inches. The roots are tough and persistent, and extremely hard to eradicate. The leaves are dull green, matte, sharply toothed, and covered in hairs, which break off when touched, leaving formic acid and a burning sensation on the skin. The greenish-yellow flowers are minute and insignificant, and are carried in curving trusses like miniature catkins.

CULTIVATION

No one ever plants nettles: they just arrive, and they come to stay. All you need to start a colony is a piece of root with an eye.

HOW TO USE

The young leaves are good lightly cooked like spinach, and in soup garnished with croûtons and cream. They are also used to make beer.

In self-help medicine, the leaves were used to treat rheumatism, as a diuretic, and as a soothing aid to skin problems.

The root fiber was at one time used to make twine, and bunches of fresh leaves were hung in the home to deter flies.

Above:

Young stinging nettle leaves are used to make beer, and are lightly cooked as spinach. They are delicious both as a vegetable and in soup.

Above left:

Nettles, which grow as a vigorous and rampant weed, are attractive to bees and butterflies and are frequently grown for this reason.

Left:

Vervain leaves have no culinary uses but may be made into a tisane which is a soothing bedtime drink and may help to alleviate nervous conditions.

Verbena officinalis

VERVAIN

THE YELLOWISH-GREEN LEAVES WITH A FOLKLORIC
REPUTATION AS A LOVE POTION AND, MORE RECENTLY,
AS AN INGREDIENT IN LIQUEURS: AN INFUSION OF THE
LEAVES TAKEN IN SELF-HELP MEDICINE TO ACT AS A
MILD SEDATIVE . . .

A native of the Mediterranean region, vervain now grows wild on waste ground and by the wayside in Europe and North America. Although it has no culinary uses, it has a long history of medicinal applications, particularly in the treatment of nervous disorders.

HISTORY

The plant was once considered virtually a cure-all, as well as a powerful aphrodisiac, and Culpeper listed many claimed remedies in his herbal. Vervain was also associated with witchcraft and believed to have magical powers.

IDENTIFICATION

A herbaceous perennial, vervain grows to a height of 3 feet and may be 18 inches across. It has fibrous, spreading roots and hairy, branching stems. The yellowish-green, toothed leaves are up to about 2 inches long. The flowers, borne at the tips of the shoots, are small, purple, and insignificant.

CULTIVATION

Vervain is grown from seed planted in spring or from tip cuttings taken in summer. The roots can be divided in spring or fall. It likes a good, well-drained soil and plenty of sun.

HOW TO USE

The tisane made from the fresh or dried leaves is a mild sedative, a soothing bedtime drink. The infusion may be taken to alleviate nervous conditions and depression, and to aid digestion. In self-help medicine, a diluted infusion was used as an eye bath to sooth inflamed and sore eyes.

Right:

Vervain, which forms a dense, compact plant, likes a good, well-drained soil and plenty of sun.

Index

Page numbers in *italics* represent illustrations.

PICTURE CREDITS

KEY *l* = left, *r* = right, *t* = top, *b* = bottom

British Library, London: p6; **Liz Eddison:** p15*(r);* **ET Archive:** p7; **Iris Hardwick Library:** p8, 10, 20*(r),* 22, 23, 25, 28, 29, 30, 35*(t);* **The Lindley Library:** 16, 18*(l),* 32; **R W Peplow:** p35*(b);* **Quarto Publishing:** illustrations p13, 20–28, 30 by Lorraine Harrison, Trevor Wood p56, 58, 86, 98*(b),* 102, 105, 110, 123, Tim Hill p62, 67, 113, Clive Corless p93, John Heseltine p68, Paul Forrester p11, 12, 14, Nelson Hargreaves 18*(r),* 32*(r),* 33, 34, 36–52; **The Royal Horticultural Society:** p20*(l);* **Harry Smith Collection:** p15*(l),* 17, 98*(t),* 124.